Confidence
to be **Yourself**

Dʀ BRIAN ROET

The
Confidence
to be Yourself

HOW TO

BOOST YOUR

SELF-ESTEEM

Foreword by **Claire Rayner**

PIATKUS

*For those whose lives would be so much
happier with a little more confidence*

PIATKUS

First published in Great Britain in 1998 by Piatkus Books
This paperback edition published in 1998 by Piatkus Books

Copyright © Dr Brian Roet 1998

Reprinted 1999 (twice), 2000 (three times), 2001, 2002, 2003 (twice),
2005, 2007

The moral right of the author has been asserted

A CIP catalogue record for this book
is available from the British Library

ISBN 978-0-7499-1926-9

Printed and bound in Great Britain by
Mackays of Chatham Ltd, Chatham, Kent

Piatkus Books
An imprint of
Little, Brown Book Group
100 Victoria Embankment
London EC4Y 0DY

An Hachette Livre UK Company

www.piatkus.co.uk

Contents

Acknowledgements

I would like to thank Rekha for all the support she has given me and the wonderful way she could interpret my hieroglyphics and convert them into orderly manuscript.

I would also like to thank Katherine who helped me improve my school-boy grammar and reminded me of such strange words as past participle and pluperfect.

And lastly, I would like to thank all the clients whose quests and queries stimulated my desire to understand that ubiquitous word – confidence.

A man found an eagle's egg and put it in a nest of a barnyard hen. The eaglet hatched with the brood of chicks and grew up with them.

All his life the eagle did what the barnyard chicks did, thinking he was a barnyard chicken. He scratched the earth for worms and insects. He clucked and cackled. And he would thrash his wings and fly a few feet into the air.

Years passed and the eagle grew very old. One day he saw a magnificent bird above him in the cloudless sky. It glided in graceful majesty among the powerful wind currents, with scarcely a beat of its strong golden wings.

The old eagle looked up in awe. 'Who's that?' he asked.

'That's the eagle, the king of the birds,' said his neighbour. 'He belongs to the sky. We belong to the earth – we're chickens.' So the eagle lived and died a chicken, for that's what he thought he was.

Anthony de Mello
AWARENESS

Foreword

I will never forget my first meeting with Brian Roet. I knew a bit about him – that he was a doctor of medicine, that he was Australian, that he had been a very gifted footballer playing for his city, and that he had an interest in helping people learn to live happily with their lives in their world. But no more than that. I didn't know what his techniques were, for example, or what his philosophy might be.

His consulting rooms were, I have to say, unusual. There was a great deal to look at in pictures on the walls, oddments on desks, and so on. But what riveted me was the clock over the mantelpiece

It looked like an ordinary round-faced, black-numbered school or hospital clock, the sort of institutional item we've all grown up with. But there was something odd about it and it took me a moment or two to work out what it was. And then I realised it was going backwards.

Try to imagine it. A clock that doesn't run clockwise. A clock that at 4 pm seems to say 8 pm.

I asked him why on earth he had such a weird clock and he told me it was a tool for a happier life.

'Look at it,' he said 'and don't try to work out what the time is by counting the hours or anything technical like that. Just let your mind flip over, as it were, to see the clock the other way round.'

Well, I tried and at first I couldn't make any sense of it. And then suddenly, just as I was beginning to think this was a load of rubbish, it happened. My mind did 'flip over' and I could tell the time quite easily, round the other way. It was a bit like those so called 'magic-eye pictures' which you look at with your eyes glazed and unfocused, and out of the mass of scribble and colour a three-dimensional figure appears.

What is the point of this story? A very important one. Looking at Brian Roet's clock made me think differently, reminded me that there is always another way of looking at any situation, dilemma or life crisis – and that to let my mind 'flip over' and find that other way was route to a better, more relaxed life.

This book is very like that clock. If you read it (and it's very easy to read – he has a lovely comfortable style, has Brian Roet!) and let its ideas slip into your mind and then act on them, you will find that you can be a different person. You many think you lack self-confidence but it's in there somewhere, deep inside you. Brian's book will help you release it. And if you ever doubt that, as you read, remember that clock that goes backwards. You can change anything you want to, you see things differently the way this book does.

Claire Rayner

Introduction

There are many books in the book shops stating they will make you confident enough to be a brain surgeon or astronaut in six weeks. This is not one of them.

The aim of this book is to explore confidence and explain what it actually means. During this process of exploration you will discover aspects of your own confidence and learn ways to improve it.

The chapters are arranged to guide you through this process of exploration and discovery. Firstly, we look at what confidence actually is, and ways to assess your own specific confidence; then we look at the different components and how alteration of these can improve confidence; then we will explore the role confidence plays in our everyday lives.

I have been a therapist for 20 years and seen thousands of clients during that time. Whatever the problem was that caused them to seek my advice, somewhere hidden in their attitude and behaviour was a lack of confidence, low self-esteem.

The writing in the following pages is given from my point of view. I am more logical than emotional so the facts stated will be more of an analytical factual nature than emotional. I have used the vast data from my clients and also from myself – I see the client and therapist being of the same mould.

Of necessity, the case histories are abbreviated and it may seem that change has occurred in a simple and easy way. This is not so. Confidence building occurs step by step. Often it is two steps forward and one back. The aim is to *learn* during the process of improvement. The people who benefited most were those who were motivated, took responsibility and put time and effort into getting better. They were prepared to make mistakes, take risks and face their fears. As one client once said, 'I am a very lucky person. It is strange that the harder I work the luckier I become.'

In every case that I can recall my clients' fears turned out to be much less than they believed once they were faced.

Read the book slowly. Don't race through it just so you can add it to the pile of self-help books in your bookcase. Focus on yourself and your needs, so you can relate the case histories and explanations to your specific difficulties. Realise that people take time to mature and your attitudes and learning will take time to change too.

This book is like a cookbook or gardening manual. They don't make the meals or grow the plants for you. Similarly, this book will provide the information you need to help you develop confidence, but it won't do it for you. The process is like making a cake – you need a number of ingredients, perhaps trial and error, and the ability to learn from your mistakes.

At the end of each chapter are lists of confidence boosters. As you read them make a decision to put one or two into practice. Create an attitude of 'having a go'. Your confidence will grow mainly from experience, not theory, so have some experience and learn from it. You need repetition, practise and mistakes to help you.

Purchase an exercise book to be a companion to this book. Make notes of your thoughts as you read. Use the exercise book to write the exercises at the end of the chapters so you can reflect on them. Any sayings or experiences that you learn can be recorded like a diary; in this way you are reinforcing the confidence-building process.

The process of confidence building begins and ends with you. Learning the steps in this process makes it that much easier. Why make your road to confidence an unpleasant journey? Why not focus on it as a learning process you can enjoy. It is your journey, made by your choice with a greatly beneficial outcome.

I really enjoyed writing this book, learning about confidence and myself at the same time. I do hope you enjoy reading it.

Section One

UNDERSTANDING CONFIDENCE

1

What is Confidence?

The dictionary defines confidence as a 'feeling of reliance or certainty, a sense of self-reliance'. The word is derived from the Latin *confido* – 'to put one's faith or trust in someone'. Confidence therefore means we put faith and trust in ourselves.

Secure is derived from the Latin word *securus* which means 'carefree'. The word 'sure' is a telescoped version of 'secure'. Insecure (the opposite of confident) means the opposite of carefree, that is instead of being free of care, we are overwhelmed by it. Other descriptions that may apply to this state of mind are low self-esteem, shy, frightened.

But these are all labels. This book will explore what lies behind these labels we so glibly use. In the process you will discover what confidence actually means to you.

The feeling of confidence is aimed in two directions which are intertwined. Confidence in oneself is reflected by our confidence in external situations. Our exploring pathway, of necessity, needs to go inside to understand how we function as well as outside to study how we cope with the situations we encounter.

My information mainly comes from people with insecurity and the ways they gain confidence, so the perspective will be from studying problems and their solutions, but in fact the chapters ahead are for *everyone* – no matter who they are or what they do – as confidence is an integral component of how we all cope with life.

As confidence, or lack of it, means something different to each individual, it is for you the reader to translate the following chapters into your own personal needs. A common comment I hear is, 'I really am insecure but everyone thinks I'm the most confident person at work. I'm amazed and bewildered why they think that when I am obviously not.'

So often what appears to be confidence can be insecurity in disguise. Behind the apparent confidence can be someone feeling frightened and shy, too frightened to admit to themselves how they feel. Be wary if you are comparing yourself unfavourably with someone else, you may *both* be saying 'I wish I could be as confident as he is.'

Lack of confidence hides behind the mask of arrogance, bullying, aggressiveness, supreme optimism and many other so-called 'confident' attitudes. It may be concealed behind the workaholic, the perfectionist or the extrovert who are all using energy and activity to prevent others and themselves facing their insecurity. The fat jolly person may well have built that physical attitude as a defence against the outer world. The gorgeously thin model, too, may be disguising her shyness and anorexia in a socially acceptable way.

All this demonstrates that confidence is a chameleon and exploring it is not a straightforward matter. It is essential to happiness and its loss causes pain and hardship, from the shy schoolboy to the much-married adult.

The quest of this book is to learn *what* it is, *what causes us to lose it* and *what we can do to build it up*. The journey will touch on many other aspects of our lives to provide a broader perspective on how they function. When you reach the end of the book you will know a lot more about this feeling which is simply called confidence.

As you go through life make this your goal,
Keep your eye upon the doughnut and not upon the hole.
                    DOUGHNUT CAFÉ, MELBOURNE

CONFIDENCE BOOSTERS

- There are many ways to assess confidence:
  - Being able to perform specific tasks.
    'I know I have confidence because I find it easy to ask a girl for a date.'
  - Relating confidence to a feeling.
    'When my confidence is strong – high, I feel like bursting out of my skin.'
  - Depending on the opinion of others.
    'Tom thinks I'm just great and that boosts my confidence immensely.'
  - Reflecting on past performances.
    'I feel really confident about going for that job because I did so well in my A levels.'

Your own assessment questions

- How would you assess your confidence?
- Does it vary or is it stable no matter what situation you are in?
- Using a scale of A = high, B = average, C = low, how would you rate an assessment of your confidence by:
  - Your boss
  - Your friends
  - Your workmates
- What factors alter your confidence? Do you find that you learn from experience, ie. you are more confident with repeated situations, or are you uninfluenced by the fact that you have had similar experiences previously?
- Does someone else's support improve your confidence?
- Do you constantly compare the way you feel to how you imagine other people feel?

2

Do We Learn Confidence or Are We Born With It?

Is the 'basic state' of humans positive; one of confidence and self-assurance or is it one of insecurity and vulnerability?

Are we born confident and lose it owing to our experiences, or is the reverse true? Are we born vulnerable, building up confidence as we grow?

Observing a baby we see a creature who is dependent, vulnerable and frightened of change. The baby may be basically happy and content but responds to new experiences with concern and fear.

Looking at the animal kingdom some animals rarely show confidence – mice and rabbits are continually alert to the danger of predators. Lions, on the other hand, appear to be born with confidence, realise their power and assume their dominant role over other animals. The difference between these species is one of power – the mouse realises it has no power and relies on alertness and speed to survive; the lion is aware of its power and radiates this knowledge so that other species respect its attitude. The mouse is not in control, the lion is.

The lion has a genetic disposition supported by experience that creates an attitude of self-confidence; the mouse with its genetic make-up and knowledge of its vulnerability does not use confidence as a survival mechanism.

When we discuss 'genetic' versus 'acquired' reasons for our behaviour, perhaps confidence is a combination of both. We are born with the *potential* for confidence but need nurturing parents to bring it to fruition. If our parents were not the loving, supporting, praising kind, our build up of confidence is delayed until we achieve positive experiences in adulthood.

We need to overcome the mouse-like tendencies that are part of our childhood, overcome fears, take risks, learn from mistakes rather than avoid them.

Imagine an ill-treated dog rescued by caring owners from the Battersea Dogs' Home. It needs to update its internal information and re-learn values with its new owners to reach its true potential.

This updating process is based on four factors:

- facing fears
- learning to trust – others and itself
- taking risks
- learning from its own experience

Using the dog as a model we can learn a great deal. The dog learnt many things from its original owners, things necessary for survival:

- It has no control.
- It needs to be frightened and on guard.
- It cannot trust its owners (or anyone else).
- It cannot trust its own feelings/instincts.
- Life is frightening, painful and confusing.
- Life is a tightrope, one wrong step and pain results.
- The world is a confusing place, any attempts to make sense of it result in failure.
- The world is a dangerous place.

This is quite a list of things to alter with its new owner. Stored in its memory are many experiences that need to fade so that positive ones can replace them. Because survival is so important, protective devices useful in the past are slow to leave the system. Confidence and security appear little by little, by trial and error, courage and risk.

The new process of learning is completely at odds with early experience. There are two aspects of this learning:

1. That it is a normal dog.
2. The world is a safe place.

Little by little, experience by experience, in the supporting hands of its new owners the dog hopefully learns these two essential facts. As it does so the tightrope widens and becomes more supportive. It is allowed mistakes and trial and error to learn about itself and its new world. Understanding and support replace punishment and abuse. Respect and appreciation of the dog's individuality allow confidence to grow.

The same applies to humans. In order to convert our self-esteem from potential to reality, we need external nurturing to help us nurture ourselves.

As in the animal kingdom, confidence can be rapidly drained by experience.

Sarah is a 25-year-old salesgirl. She lives with her boyfriend and coped well with life until six months before her consultation when while walking home from work her bag was snatched by a man hiding in the bushes.

She was thrown to the ground, received bruises and was badly shaken. She was interviewed by the police, examined by her GP and sent home.

Since that day she has been a different woman. She is scared to go out, cannot go back to work, needs someone with her when shopping, cries incessantly and is frightened of going to sleep because of nightmares.

How could this incident cause such a change in Sarah's personality? Her confidence was high before the attack and now it was zero. What happened in Sarah's mind to completely destroy her image of the world and its safety?

Sarah appeared to have changed overnight and has remained that way ever since. Her confidence had not grown in spite of the support and protection from her boyfriend and other friends.

During our initial consultation I learnt that Sarah's early life bore a striking similarity to our dog at Battersea Dogs' Home. Her parents were alcoholics and the household was a scene of abuse, fights, broken plates and furniture, police visits, neighbourhood complaints, terror and tears.

Aged 16, Sarah could take no more and left home to live with a girlfriend and her family. This house was calm and friendly, everyone treated each other with respect. Sarah found it very strange and confusing. She expected the walls to fall in at any time.

As the weeks passed, the calmness and security had a healing effect on Sarah's nerves. She started to feel and allowed a little trust to enter her life. She got a job behind the counter of a local shop and gradually lowered her guard. She met a boy who treated her well, even though she was always expecting him to revert to her father's behaviour.

She was accepted by a group of friends and her boyfriend became a trusted ally. She shared her thoughts and feelings with him and he with her. She began to see a different world where she could trust herself and others.

Then her bag was snatched and in those few seconds her world tumbled down. It was as if her supports were not strong and gave way with the terror that took over as she was hurled to the ground. Security was replaced by the confusion of her childhood. Her survival mechanisms of fear, suspicion and mistrust took over. She knew she was mistaken to trust anyone – especially men – and withdrew into her shell, wary of anything or anyone who had the potential to hurt her. Her confidence had been a veneer swept away by the attack revealing the bare boards of fear beneath.

All the hard work of many years was disrupted on that day. It was as if she had been reduced to childhood, as if she was back to square one in a game of snakes and ladders.

She was not open to any counselling or support and spent the first few sessions in tears. All she could manage was to cry, shake with fear and hold her head down. Sarah took many months to allow me into her world of fear. She required absolute reassurance she would not be let down yet again. Any holiday I took set her back as her unconscious mind read that as another rejection. If I kept her waiting more than one minute she was hostile; she tested me constantly.

Eventually she was able to lessen her doubts and fears. She made tentative forays from her home on her own. Her confidence crept up millimetre by millimetre with the continued support of her boyfriend and eventually she was able to make use of the bag-snatching experience to add to her confidence, to realise she *could* cope with a similar experience should it occur.

Potential

We are all born with our individual potential to be the best we can be. That doesn't mean we could all be prime ministers or opera singers. It means we have a 'birthright' to grow and expand our abilities and experiences to achieve what is available to us.

Confidence is an essential ingredient in achieving our potential. How often have we looked back and regretted things we didn't achieve because of lack of confidence. How small those consequences seem when we look back from the vantage point of maturity. So many things we would have done if only we had the confidence.

Instead of focusing on difficulties, problems, fears and hurdles, I would like you to focus on *your potential*. What *you* are *capable* of doing or being. I would like you to start in a practical way by listing the abilities that make up your potential, qualities that could be transformed into action, reality, achievement. By making this list you are starting the process of converting the ugly duckling into the beautiful swan. Head the list:

I am capable of doing these things (my potential). The items on the list are *your* potential, nobody else's and nobody else can achieve them for you.

The second part of the exercise is to make a commitment to actually doing one of the activities on the list every week. In this way you will be growing into your potential. It may be difficult, it may be easy, but as it is within your ability you can do it.

In the future you will look back at these tasks and realise how easy they would have been. Make use of this future perspective by doing them in the present.

Confidence helps you achieve your potential; achieving your potential helps your confidence. It is a cycle of energy (see Chapter 7 Confidence As Energy), and by entering the cycle you will be lifted up and carried forward by the energy. Forward towards what you deserve. Forward to your potential.

So the question of whether confidence is a birthright or an acquired ability is still unanswered. One thing is for certain – early nurturing is required to start the process of building confidence.

Secondly, the responsibility for achieving our potential falls on our own shoulders. It is no use continually blaming childhood for adult failures. We can build our own confidence step by step by realising our capabilities, overcoming the hurdles we find along the way and accepting the challenges as an integral part of growing up.

To achieve what you never have achieved
Do what you have never done.

CONFIDENCE BOOSTERS

- During your lifetime a number of factors played a role
  - in increasing your confidence
  - reducing your confidence
  Some experiences where you succeeded, were praised or felt good about what happened would be placed into category (1). Category (2) may relate to criticisms, apparent failures or times in your life when you felt alone or judged. Write down experiences that illustrate (1) and (2) involving parents, teachers, siblings or classmates that you recall and believe played a role in affecting your confidence.
- Think about role models you had as you grew up – parents, siblings, teachers, classmates, filmstars, public figures – and note what role they played in your present attitudes and beliefs.
- If you know your grandparents, look to them to learn about the genetic component of your confidence. Otherwise, what levels of confidence do your aunts, uncles, cousins have? Sometimes the supportive role of nurturing, or lack of it, may have been an influence. If this was the case, which relative was most prominent?

3

The Language of Confidence

Jean-Paul Sartre said, 'Words are loaded pistols'. These pistols point in two directions. One is inside you – self-talk; the second is directed at others – communication.

Both pistols reflect our confidence, causing it to be high or low. What we tell ourselves creates feelings and attitudes. What we tell others reflects our internal dialogue.

Internal Language

Observe mothers and babies and you will see mothers trying to teach babies different words. This is the beginning of learning to speak. It is also the process of developing an internal tape-recording that talks to us for the rest of our lives. As we grow we learn more and more phrases to put on the tape, how to direct ourselves, our self-talk.

If we had critical, judging and blaming parents, we create a tape that does just that. We talk to ourselves at an unconscious level and repeat what we learnt. We 'internalise' our parents' tuition and continue where they left off.

If we had supportive, caring and praising parents who respected our individuality, we develop a positive self-talking tape helping us throughout our lives.

We receive a form of brainwashing in our youth and whether it is positive or negative makes all the difference. Research has shown that by the time we reach adulthood we have 25,000 hours of parent tapes in our minds!

Consider two hypothetical people Mr A and Mr B.

Mr A had loving supporting parents, while Mr B was constantly criticised and told he was no good.

Mr A and Mr B apply for the same job, they have the same qualifications and ability.

The internal tape of Mr A as he waits for the interview is:

'I've got as good a chance as anyone. I've done well in the past and I'll do the best I can. If I don't get this job there are plenty more I can apply for but I've got a good feeling I'll succeed here.'

Mr B's self-talk is:

'Why do I waste my time with these interviews? I have no hope with all those applicants. Why do I always have such trouble with interviews? If I fail here I may as well give up and go on the dole. I'll never get a job, I just know it.'

The difference in confidence between Mr A and Mr B is largely due to their self-talk. They talk themselves into or out of success. There is a constant monologue repeating itself in their heads, creating the direction of their actions and attitudes.

When they are in the interview their internal language will be reflected in what they say and how they say it. Mr A will give positive vibrations to the interviewers while Mr B will radiate negativity, self-doubt and failure.

Our minds are divided into two components – the conscious part which we use to control and analyse and which follows our direction, and the unconscious part which influences our lives in a manner beyond our control.

An interesting fact is that the unconscious mind cannot process negative words. It has no way of dealing with them in

MR 'A' WILL GIVE POSITIVE VIBRATIONS TO THE
INTERVIEWERS WHILE MR. 'B' WILL RADIATE NEGATIVITY,
SELF-DOUBT AND FAILURE ..

our self-talk. It cannot follow an order from the conscious mind
to 'not do something'.

If you say to yourself 'Don't think of your nose', what happens? You actually *think* of your nose because your unconscious mind heard 'think of your nose' – it couldn't make sense of the negative word 'don't'.

A 12-year-old girl once came to see me with problems of bed-wetting.

'What are you doing to try and help?' I asked her.

'Oh. I say to myself 20 times "I must not wet my bed" before I go to sleep.'

Her mind was hearing, 'I must ... wet my bed' and it obliged!

I suggested she say to herself, 'I would like to have a dry bed' each night and over a period of time she did.

Many people focus on avoiding what they do not want – a double negative approach.

'I must not eat so much in order to lose weight.' This approach focuses the unconscious mind on the act of eating – exactly the opposite of what is desired. Using positive words, 'I will make sure I exercise every day and eat the nourishing foods that are best for my body' is a positive way to direct the unconscious mind.

'Won't it be terrible if I fail to get the job?' is a less successful approach than, 'It will be really great when I get the job.' People use the double negative because they believe it will avoid disappointment if they fail. By preparing themselves for failure they feel they will be less upset if it occurs.

The important thing to learn is to avoid negative words when talking to yourself. Much of our conversation consists of double negatives to create a positive.

- As Joanne waits for her new boyfriend to pick her up she tells herself, 'I hope I don't look too awful, he may run away as soon as he sees me.'
- Tom is running in a race and tells himself, 'I hope I don't fall over.'
- Sue is frightened of travelling by Tube and tells herself, 'I hope I don't have a panic attack.'

All these negative commands help to *create* what is to be avoided.

As we all have self-talk it is worth learning the correct vocabulary that is both helpful and encouraging. Learn positive words, repeating them so they come naturally and replace the previously negative ones.

One phrase that is helpful is 'It will be wonderful when . . .' This focuses your mind on positive outcomes and provides energy and enthusiasm for what you are trying to achieve.

It is like the glass filled to half full with water, you can either say, 'I'm sad because my glass is half empty', or, 'I'm glad my glass is half full'!

A very good saying and attitude which I believe to be true is: 'We do the best we can with the choices we have.'

When looking back with hindsight we *may* have done better but *at the time* we did the best we could.

As we do the best with the choices we have, we will do better if we choose positive self-talk instead of negative.

Like the donkey with the stick and carrot. If the owner only uses the stick, the donkey will not budge and be labelled 'stubborn'. Adding the carrot makes all the difference.

The *actual words* we tell ourselves have power. Choosing more suitable words can overcome obstacles and improve our confidence in the process.

'I hate confrontations. I'm dreading seeing my boss to confront him with the fact that I need a day off to visit my mother.'

The word '*confront*' has images of fighting, warfare, winning and losing, pain and humiliation. When we say it to ourselves we are implying all these terrible things.

Changing the word to '*negotiate*' has a completely different internal effect. It allows rationality, bargaining, discussing, putting different points of view, remaining friendly, etc., to be associated with the task ahead.

Going to see the boss to *negotiate* a day off to visit mother has a completely different feeling to seeing the boss to *confront* him about a day off. Checking the effect words have on you allows you to choose similar words that are less restrictive.

We learn our internal language just as we learn a foreign language. Changing from negative to positive is just like learning a new language.

Begin by writing all the negative words you tell yourself – all the negative ways you give yourself a hard time.

Let us use Deborah as an example. She came to see me because her relationships always collapsed after a few months and she knew it was because of her attitude.

We discussed her internal self-talk and the comments she told herself were:

- I'm not pretty, I'm overweight, my nose is too long.
- I'm no good at doing things.
- I'm not interesting.
- I'll only get a partner by going to bed with him on the first night.
- I'm not intelligent.
- Life isn't fair.
- Everyone has a better time than I do.

Her internal conversation was very negative and she radiated this to everyone she met.

We spent a number of sessions focusing on the things she *was* good at. It was like extracting teeth but eventually we formulated a small list:

- I'm kind and thoughtful.
- I love animals.
- I work hard.
- I like rock music.
- I'm honest.

I then asked Deborah to repeat her new vocabulary like a mantra. She was also to talk to her best friend and ask what she liked about Deborah. (It was very difficult getting her to do this.)

Over a period of time she was to note the *good* things that happened to her each day, and focus on those.

Deborah certainly improved her life by changing her vocabulary. She was able to go to dances and parties without sitting in the corner sulking about how the world was unfair.

Self-talk is the continuous tape running in our minds as we talk to ourselves in a variety of ways. Sometimes we are advisers, criticisers, judges, praisers, blamers – one part is speaking to another.

To improve confidence we need to converse with ourselves as a friend, a good parent, a supportive helper.

To obtain the optimum benefit from self-talk, we need to:

- be aware of the internal tape
- ensure it is in our best interests
- have it up to date and appropriate
- have it in a form that is acceptable

There are two ways of improving self-talk and both can be used.

1. Be aware of the way you talk to yourself and make sure it is:
   - not negative
   - up to date and suitable
   - in a form that is acceptable
2. Make a specific exercise each day to improve your internal vocabulary.

This requires giving yourself quiet time to focus on your self-talk. This quiet time enhances the effect and speeds up the process of change.

You can use this time to reflect in a positive way about the events of the last 24 hours. I call this 'Panning for Gold' as it resembles the miner looking in his dish full of mud for the specks of gold. His focus is not on the mud – he knows that is there, but does not need to pay attention to it – it is on the few shining specks that catch his eye.

In the same way, focusing on good things that have happened during the day allows a positive and praising dialogue to develop in your mind.

The other way to utilise this quiet time is to repeat 'affirmations' to yourself.

These affirmations are succinct phrases used to improve our self-talk. There are many books containing affirmations and it is important to choose those that suit your attitude to life. There are also tapes of affirmations which may be used as a framework for your quiet time.

As you are going through the process of improving your self-talk, compliment yourself on the fact that you are doing something that will help your confidence.

So often the words we use are negative even though this is not our intention.

'I'd love to see Rocky IV.'

'*Don't be so stupid*. It's just for kids.'

Although the other person didn't mean it, the phrase 'don't be so stupid' is hardly complimentary or accepting of the first speaker.

'I really liked that play we saw.'

'*You must be crazy*. They couldn't act at all.'

These phrases are common in our language and as words are loaded pistols we are constantly shooting anyone within earshot. This criticism undermines the *whole process* not just their attitude or remarks and as such is destructive and unnecessary.

It's a Question of Confidence

The asking of questions is often linked to insecurity. Some people only converse by asking questions. You may know someone who ends every comment with a question mark. The reason for this may be lack of confidence. Questions do many things:

Create a defence mechanism

By using questions the focus of attention is projected on to the listener. This provides a safe haven for the questioner away from the spotlight. Insecurities are thus protected and cannot be criticised as no statement has been made.

By asking questions we feel safe from judgement.

Give control to the listener

As insecure people desire control but dread the responsibility of it, they achieve this aim by asking questions. Once a question is asked the control is with the receiver. Often mothers who are having difficulty with their children resort to questioning as a means of communication. This generally makes matters worse as the child realises he is in control.

Avoid responsibility

Answering a question with a question helps to deflect responsibility away from the speaker. In a restaurant I have observed the waiter asking a woman what she would like and her turning to her husband and asking, 'What is it I like, dear?'

A husband and wife came to see me for pain relief for her arthritis.

'And where is the pain?' I asked her.

She turned to her husband, 'John, where does it hurt?'

'In your left knee, dear.'

'Oh yes. My left knee is very painful.'

That woman didn't even take responsibility for knowing where her pain was.

Making a statement causes many people to feel vulnerable. In their eyes they are open to criticism and blame. Hiding behind questions provides the refuge that is so desperately sought by the insecure.

In a book called *Your Best Year Yet* by J. Ditzler, I discovered *the cycle of productivity*. It is a simple way of putting positive energy into the things you do.

It can apply to *anything* you do from brushing your teeth to applying for a job.

There are four steps:

1. Think of what you want to do.
2. Start doing it.
3. Finish it.
4. Praise yourself for what you did.

The fourth step is the most important. Most people do steps 1, 2, 3 then back to 1. Some do 1, 2, 3 then tell themselves they did it badly, they are hopeless or some such critical comment.

Anytime you do something add step 4. Develop this into a habit. Each time you do so you will be increasing your confidence.

The language of confidence comes in many forms. Converting negative into positive self-talk; using positive words when talking to others; focusing on positive outcomes; using the productivity cycle all help to make your internal dialogue a friend and ally.

The most important words you'll ever hear
are those you tell yourself.

CONFIDENCE BOOSTERS

- Internal language is often reflected in the way we speak externally. The words you use, your tone of voice and rate at which you speak may all give clues to the tapes playing in your unconscious mind.

    Be aware of your external language, note self-critical, praising, or guilt-laden words. These words may well filter through from the unconscious.
- How often do you call yourself hopeless, stupid, lazy, etc.? Would you say it was
    - often
    - occasionally
    - never?

    Choose some positive, praising words that you could practise to describe yourself – eg. kind, assertive, creative, hard-working, like-able, successful, healthy, friendly, enthusiastic, have a good sense of humour, fair, well-balanced, etc. Ensure you use some of these words every day when talking to yourself or to others.
- Purchase a tape of affirmations (see Further Reading) that suits your character and play it daily until the phrases become second nature.
- Practise the cycle of productivity after any action you perform. Remember to use step 4 by praising yourself after completing the action.

4

That Confident Feeling

Confidence is like a jigsaw made up of many pieces. The first of these is *feeling*. This feeling of confidence is a complex one connected to thoughts and rationality – but a feeling nevertheless.

- Where in our body is this feeling called confidence? What is the feeling called lack of confidence? Is it just an absence of the confident feeling?
- Is confidence kept in our stomach, our chest, our minds?
- Does it have a shape or colour?
- Is it hot, cold, tingly, light, dark?
- Is it heavy, light, tense, relaxed?

By learning more about this feeling we can gain some control over it and build it up when it is lacking.

Paul was a 45-year-old car salesman who had 'lost his nerve', was off sick and 'couldn't face another customer'. He looked unhappy, down in the dumps and tense as he came into my consulting room. All his body language was telling me he was suffering.

'Doctor, I've lost my confidence. I used to be able to sell cars in my sleep; now when a customer comes into the salesroom I start to shake and have to take a Valium. I never used to be like this, I was one of the most confident salesmen at work.'

During the session I asked Paul specifically about the feeling he called confidence.

'I used to feel good. I had a spring in my step and a light feeling in my chest. It was as if I didn't have a care. I knew I could sell cars so it was no problem.'

'How did you know that, Paul?' I asked.

'I just knew it, I felt it in my bones, I had a good feeling in my chest telling me I'm good at the job.'

'And what feeling do you have now when you see a client in the showroom?'

'Oh. It feels terrible. I feel like I want to run away; I feel I'll fail and the boss will get angry.'

'What happened to that feeling in your chest?'

Paul became confused. 'What do you mean? Oh, that feeling in my chest, it's not like that anymore. It feels dark and heavy and shaky in there.'

As the story unravelled it became apparent why Paul's confidence had left him.

Over the previous year Paul had gone through a destructive divorce. Then when he was starting to get over the trauma, his boss left and a new critical one was installed. Paul was judged and blamed for things that went wrong in the office; 'the good feelings about myself' were replaced with anxiety, fear, doubts and loss of confidence.

For Paul confidence was represented by:

- 'a light feeling in my chest'
- 'a spring in my step'
- 'a knowledge I am a good salesman'
- 'a feeling in my bones'

When events drained this feeling it was replaced by lack of confidence:

- 'a terrible feeling'

- 'I want to run away'
- 'I feel I'll fail and make the boss angry'
- 'a dark, heavy feeling in my chest'
- 'a shaky, frightened feeling'

At one end of the spectrum is confidence, at the other insecurity and fear. The aim of therapy is to help clients move from the fear end of the spectrum to the confident one.

Step 1 in the process is to learn as much as you can about the feeling you call confidence (or lack of it). There are many ways to tackle this process and at many different levels. Paul needed to undo the damage caused by the divorce and learn how to deal with his critical manager without fear. Many times he commented on the catch-22 situation: 'If I had confidence I would automatically deal with the manager differently.' I replied that this was true and also if he *took a risk* and dealt with his manager with less fear his confidence would return. He was caught in a cycle being maintained by fear.

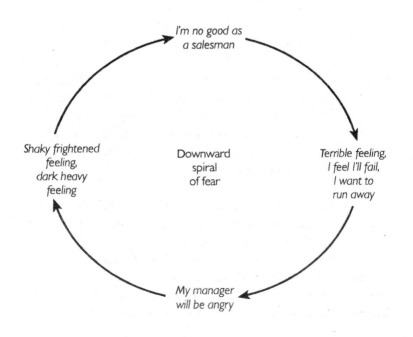

Each incident that revolved the cycle depleted Paul of more confidence. The aim of therapy was to help Paul replace this cycle with:

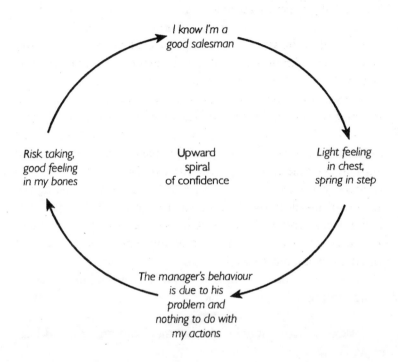

Over a period of months Paul was able to disassociate himself from the manager's problems. He noticed the manager was angry and critical of all the other (more successful) salesmen and so Paul was able to let the manager's outbursts pass him by.

As he made a few sales we were able to use these experiences to help build his confidence and focus his attentions on positive outcomes.

It took time and many ups and downs but eventually Paul was able to maintain his upward spiral of feeling better about himself and his ability to deal with life's challenges.

Paul and I worked on many levels. One of these levels was *his feelings* – his internal responses to what was happening around him. He learnt what it *felt* like to be confident and what it *felt* like to have minimal confidence and maximum fear.

Linking these feelings with rational discussions about what was happening at work and what had happened in his divorce allowed him to make improvements. It wasn't easy. Paul was reluctant to change. He was stuck in the merry-go-round of anguish and that circular momentum was dragging him down like a whirlpool.

The sessions helped him to see things from a different perspective, recognise that his boss had problems which were demonstrated by his behaviour, realise he was a good salesman and therefore would be able to be one in future, and lastly take some risks to reverse the negative downward drag.

Learning about your own feelings means you are starting to recognise a most important piece of the jigsaw.

Asking yourself where in your body or mind is the feeling you call 'confidence' starts you on that pathway of discovery.

Next ask what is it like – imagine yourself going into that part of your body – colour, shape, weight, tension, sounds, lightness or darkness, radiation and anything else you can learn about it.

I've asked many people to explore their feelings of confidence and here are some of their replies:

- 'Its like laughter in my chest: lightness and tinkling and I can hear and feel the laughter.'
- 'It's in my head. I can see my brain – strong, large, firm and powerful. When I lack confidence my brain shrinks and becomes soft and powerless.'
- 'When I'm confident, there is a garden in my stomach. It is full of flowers in bloom and it is sunny, warm and tranquil. When I lack confidence, the garden is bare and cold.'

It is possible to work with these visualisations of the feeling of confidence. Barbara's story illustrated this.

Barbara was a 50-year-old architect from Spain. She was unmarried, very nervous and lacked confidence. Her life was ruled by fear and is fraught with a myriad of problems. Her voice trembled as she told me her history. She had been brought up in foster homes and had never received an input of security. Fear had been her constant companion throughout childhood. Her move from Spain to London had opened old wounds of unstability and she was having trouble coping with her new life and job.

After many sessions I asked her, 'If you had any confidence, where would it reside in your body?'

She looked confused and I patiently explained my strange question.

'It would be in my chest,' she replied in her mouselike voice, indicating with her hand.

'I'd like you to use your imagination and go inside your chest and learn about this thing called confidence.'

She sat quietly for a minute or two then said, 'It's a small brown seed.'

After a few more minutes' silence I asked, 'What would you like to happen to the small brown seed?'

'For it to grow.'

'What would it need to help it grow?'

'Soil, water and nourishment.'

'Is there soil there?'

'Not very much.'

'Are you able to help with water and nourishment and adding more soil?'

'Yes. I think so.'

There was silence while Barbara concentrated on her internal task. Three or four minutes went by before she said, 'I'm feeling more relaxed. I'm watering the soil to make sure it is moist and protected. In a strange way, it feels better and more secure.'

'Will you spend some time each day with your seed of confidence?'

'Yes. I'll make sure I do that. Somehow I have a feeling it may help a little.'

Barbara and I worked on other aspects of her life and each time we met I asked about the 'brown seed of confidence'. Over a period of months it grew into a lovely flower. She transplanted some of the brown seeds of the flower and grew more. Her confidence increased as the flowers blossomed.

It's hard to know what actually causes improvement, but Barbara commented that her time spent nurturing the brown seed of confidence played an important role in her improvement and coping abilities.

The cases of Paul and Barbara focus on ways to 'see' our feelings. By converting feelings into pictures we can start to alter them and produce more positive attitudes. Associated with this improvement we can make our self-talk more positive, like improving the soundtrack on a film.

By focusing on these components of our feelings we can gradually gain control. Just as when we add some pieces to a jigsaw the picture is changed.

Improving each component of the feeling is a much easier way of changing than trying to tackle the feeling in its entirety.

Self-confidence is the first requisite to great undertakings.
SAMUEL JOHNSON

CONFIDENCE BOOSTERS

- In order to learn about feelings sit quietly for ten minutes each day with your eyes closed and your attention focused internally. It may take a little while to achieve this as we are used to focusing our attention externally. Don't be upset if your mind wanders, in time it will become more calm. Spend a few minutes journeying around your body noting how the different parts feel. Where is your feeling of confidence? Learn about its shape, colour, temperature, weight, etc.
- Explore your body sensations (see p.24) and note where your 'lack of confidence' feeling resides.
- During the day note times when you possess the confident feeling and times when you have the lack of confidence feeling.

- Try and alter these feelings of low confidence by changing perspective on the situation – seeing it from a more positive point of view. Note if confidence can be increased by improving your self-talk to make it more praising and less critical.

5

The Confidence to be Yourself

Confidence consists of three components:

1. The confidence to know yourself.
2. The confidence to like yourself.
3. The confidence to accept yourself.

This does not mean you are excellent at everything you do. It means you accept who you are and respect that.

I'll illustrate with two hypothetical figures.

Joe is 40 years old. He is short, five foot eight and is going bald. He runs a successful business, giving presentations and travelling a lot. He is married with two daughters.

Joe has never spent any time learning about himself; he has been too busy with his business. He is often in a bad mood, his marriage is failing, and he spends little time with his wife and daughters who fear his outbursts of temper.

Joe wears built-up shoes and has had a hair transplant. He wears expensively tailored suits and drives a very smart car. He eats at expensive restaurants where the head waiters know him and cater to his needs.

Joe constantly worries about his business. He is forever

angry with his employees and there is a constant turnover of staff. He criticises their work and blames them for any difficulties. He has become a workaholic over the last few years, going to work early and bringing work home with him. He has few hobbies and talks a lot about his business successes.

Tim is very similar to Joe in age and physical build. He too is short and losing his hair. He runs a business, is married and has two daughters.

In his twenties and thirties Tim spent a lot of time learning about himself. He read a number of self-help books, went to a therapist for a while and showed interest in Eastern attitudes to oneself. His conversation is more about people than objects.

He would rather be taller and not losing his hair but he accepts this as an unchangeable fact and is able to joke about it. He gives presentations in his business but is never comfortable with them in spite of attending courses on this subject.

He spends a lot of his spare time with his family and spends more money on holidays with them than on acquisitions.

Tim and Joe respond differently to life mainly because of the difference in their three components.

Tim knows himself, likes himself and accepts himself more than Joe does. These three qualities make all the difference in the characters, personality and attitude of these two hypothetical men.

Joe is angry – basically the anger is directed at himself but he projects it on to others. He is angry because he cannot accept who he is. He does not like who he really is. He goes 'out there' to find his happiness in acquisitions and success in business. He is more aggressive than assertive and blames others for the problems that arise. He has a 'short fuse'.

Joe's anger and aggressiveness are in reality a defence mechanism to protect his deepest darkest secret. He believes his survival depends on preventing others finding out about this secret. He is forever busy to prevent *himself* finding out too.

This secret is *that he is not a nice person*. He 'knows' this for a fact even though it is not true. He does everything in his power to hide this from himself and others. The thought of learning about himself terrifies him as it would mean coming face to face with the horrible person he believes he is.

His lack of inner peace is obvious to those around him. He radiates anger and fear. His friends and family tread cautiously when 'sensitive' subjects are discussed such as business ventures, his height or hair.

Tim, on the other hand, has nothing to hide. He has learnt about his dark side and accepts his deficiencies. He is open to discussion about any subject and is able to laugh at himself.

He accepts responsibility for his faults, he knows he is lacking in many areas and is not worried if others find out. He tries to learn from his mistakes. Blame, judgement and criticism, either of himself or others, do not play a role in his life. His tolerance level is high and he realises others are doing the best they can.

We can learn a number of things by looking at the way Joe and Tim lead their lives. The mechanism they use creates outcomes as well as providing apparent defence mechanisms.

Joe's basic anger is at himself but he 'projects' it on to others. This mechanism of projection is very common. The basis is that we tell ourselves something but project the words as if they are coming from others.

For example, I think I have a large nose. I notice someone looking at me and believe they are looking at my large nose. I tell myself, 'They think I have a large nose' when in reality it is *my* belief and not *theirs*.

Joanne is 40 and lives on her own. She is upset and embarrassed by not having a partner. I asked her if she went to the pictures at all. 'Oh. I couldn't do that, what would the people in the theatre think of me being there on my own?'

Joanne was projecting her own thoughts on to 'the people in the theatre'. Joe's belief that he is 'not a nice person' may be a 'self-fulfilling prophecy'. This means that he creates an outcome by his attitude. By telling himself he is not a nice person he may well achieve this.

We are our beliefs and even though they may be initially incorrect we steer them into a truth which in itself reinforces the belief.

THE MECHANISM OF PROJECTION IS VERY COMMON. THE BASIS IS THAT WE TELL OURSELVES SOMETHING BUT PROJECT THE WORDS AS IF THEY ARE COMING FROM OTHERS.

We all have some parts of Joe or Tim or Joanne within us. Our aim is to recognise them and ensure their attitudes and actions are in our best interests. Flexibility and openness help us more than unbending rigidity. Tim is more flexible than Joe, by being open, having little to hide, he doesn't need to build a protective fortress.

Three stories will illustrate this. The first is a Chinese parable about the bamboo and the fir tree who lived in forest together.

The fir tree was forever exclaiming how he was the king of the forest – tall and straight and regal.

'You lowly bamboo, why are you so weak, you bend with every breeze, always bowing and kow-towing. Why don't you stand straight as I do and defy the winds.'

But the bamboo didn't reply, it just rustled with the breeze and bent over to let it pass.

Then the winter came and the winds blew strongly. The branches of the rigid fir tree were broken and it cried out in pain. The bamboo bent to the ground letting the strong winds fly over it.

Then the snow came and weighed heavily on the fir tree's boughs and the weight broke them and the fir tree cried out more. The bamboo bent and the snow slid to the ground.

When the spring came the fir tree was a bedraggled creature bemoaning his fate. The bamboo stood green, straight and flexible and said nothing.

The second story I learnt when I was in India recently. I travelled around Rajasthan, a province famous for its forts. Each large town had an impressive fort built on a strategic point sur-rounded by large walls.

One town however – Udaipur – had no such fortress or walls. It was open to the plains. In previous centuries many forts had been built there and were overrun time and time again by enemies. Each time this occurred the town was looted and many of its citizens killed.

A wise leader took over Udaipur and when the townsfolk clamoured for a bigger and stronger fort he held a meeting with the elders. He pointed out the disastrous history of having each fort destroyed by the enemy and convinced them to rid the town of its treasures, leave the gates of the city open and provide hospitality to the enemies.

Since then Udaipur has lived in peace and prosperity; the only town in that area that is not surrounded by walls.

The third story is also from India.

There was a very wise guru who used to sit under a Banyan tree. People came from far and wide to hear his wisdom and to participate in the 'ceremony of enlightenment'.

He would listen to the travellers and ask them questions about their lives, what they wanted, their hopes and fears. He would nod wisely and offer a few comments. They would talk and drink tea for many hours then he would lead them across a field to a disused aeroplane hangar.

'Now you are going to experience the ceremony of enlightenment. Over there is a long aeroplane hangar. The door at this end does not have a handle on the inside so once you go in you cannot return this way.

Inside the hangar are your worst fears so the journey may be difficult. You may need to take risks and face your fears. As you journey through the building, you will be gaining enlightenment and when you reach the other end there is a door to release you into the sunshine.

I want to give you two pieces of advice to carry with you on your journey. The first is that in order to reach the other end you will need to keep moving; the second is that all the fears in there are of your own creation.'

Then he would lead the people into the hangar and close the door after them.

Our fictitious villain Joe *needed* a fortress to protect his vital secret, just as the pride of the fir tree required it to stand tall and erect. The hero Tim's fortress was his perceived weakness; like the people of Udaipur, he had nothing to hide and there was no need to build a defensive wall.

The ceremony of enlightenment does indeed point out that we create our own fears. As this is true we are capable of creating our own solutions and confidence.

By knowing ourselves, liking ourselves and accepting ourselves we can be open to the winds or enemies. The confidence that comes with this flexibility allows us to enjoy life in the best possible manner.

If you are not able to be yourself, who are you?

CONFIDENCE BOOSTERS

- In order to have confidence in yourself you need to know who you are. You are made up of many qualities some of which you may perceive to be positive, others flawed. To assess how much you like yourself write a list of qualities you regard as positive, and qualities you perceive as flawed.

- Spend some time looking at the two lists and *accept them for the time being.* Tell yourself, 'This is me for the moment; hopefully I can improve some of the flawed characteristics in the future, but for now I am doing the best I can with the resources I have.'

- Take a risk and share one of your perceived negative features with a friend. This releases energy you are using to conceal it.

6

Confidence as a Team Effort

Imagine a football team where some players believed they were kicking in one direction and other players of the same team believed they were kicking in the opposite direction.

The team wouldn't win many games. There would be fights all over the pitch and it would be more like mayhem than football.

That situation occurs in our minds every day of our life. I'm not suggesting we play football in our minds; I'm suggesting there is conflict between the different parts that make up 'ourselves'.

Take a simple example, 'I need to go to the shops, but I'm too tired.' This sentence indicates the tug-of-war inside between the part that realises if I don't go the shops there will be no food for dinner, and the part that needs a rest.

When the issue is more important, and many more parts are in conflict, then we can see how sense of purpose and achievement fall into disarray.

Alaistair was a 30-year-old male nurse. He came to see me for help with impotence. He was married at the age of 18 and had a daughter when he was 20. The relationship with his wife then began to deteriorate with many arguments and accusations. When he was 24, he left his wife and daughter in Liverpool and

came to work in a hospital in London. He still visited his wife
and daughter but each visit involved arguments and fights and
he came away feeling worse than when he went. He was not
seeking a divorce as he believed this would be wrong but he
knew there was no possibility that he and his wife would get
back together.

Over the last two years he formed a relationship with a
nurse from his hospital. This was warm, open and loving. The
only problem he had was that he was unable to sustain an
erection.

When we discussed his problem he said he realised he was
still feeling guilty about leaving his wife and child. He knew
that returning to them was not the answer and believed this
conflict may be related to his problem.

We used hypnosis to explore his unconscious mind. He
likened the situation to an army where the command was in his
mind and the privates were in his penis (private parts). When
he explored his mind he saw chaos. Everyone was giving different orders. There was no team co-ordination, some parts
were saying he should be punished; others were saying he
should go back to his wife and others that it was just too much
for them to cope with.

When he imagined going down to his penis he received the
message, 'Leave me alone; I'm going on strike. That command
centre is totally out of touch with reality.'

This imaginary scene helped Alaistair understand why he
was having sexual problems. He spent the next few months
taking pressure off himself to perform and helping the command unit to work towards the goal of living in the present
with his girlfriend.

In time things did work out well for Alaistair. He used
self-hypnosis to communicate his needs to the parts that
were previously fighting. He discussed things with his wife
and, as she suggested a divorce, he agreed. He was open
with his girlfriend about the conflicts that were occurring
inside. By doing all these things, his body returned to functioning normally.

If we are in 'two minds' about what we intend to do, our confidence will be diminished. Having the team of all our parts working together enables us to achieve our potential.

There are a variety of ways we can look upon the parts that combine to be ourselves.

1. **'I' and 'me'** 'I keep telling myself I must give up smoking but I still can't do it.'
2. **Shy and confident** 'I'm really in charge at work but, when I get home, I behave like a doormat to my husband.'
3. **Logical and emotional** 'I know it's stupid to be frightened of flying, but I feel so terrified when I try and board a plane.'
4. **Conscious and unconscious** 'I really did want to keep my appointment with you today, doctor, but I just forgot to put my alarm clock on.'
5. **Introvert and extrovert** 'I'd love to go to the party next week, but it would be so nice to have a night in on my own.'
6. **Fixer and acceptor** 'I'm forever running around doing things but I'd just love to lie down and listen to music.'

Tom was forever getting into trouble for having 'a short fuse'. His relationships suffered, he was constantly fighting and was in danger of losing his job due to his fiery temper.

When he came to see me he was a really pleasant, quiet man with fun-loving eyes and a gentle disposition.

'How come someone like you gets into fights all the time?' I asked him.

'I'm not really sure. I change if someone argues with me. I fly off the handle and before I know it all hell's broken loose.'

Tom had a lot of pent up anger from a difficult childhood and I asked him to sit quietly, close his eyes and imagine two parts of himself. One part is the Tom I was seeing in front of me, the other is the one involved in the fighting.

He sat for a while and replied slowly.

'Yes, I can see those two. One is on the right of my head, the other on the left.'

'Ask them what their names are.'

'The one on the right is the peaceful one. He is called Tom. The one on the left is seething with anger, he is Thomas.'

'Do they know each other?'

'Not really. They are vaguely aware of each others existence, that's all.'

'I'd like you to sit quietly and spend some time helping them to get to know each other. Let them know they are pulling in opposite directions with disastrous results. You would like them to work together as a team.'

Tom sat for 10 minutes in silence, then opened his eyes 'That was amazing. Did you hypnotise me?'

'Not really. I just allowed you to have time for yourself. How did it go?'

'It was amazing. I saw these two characters and I helped them get together. I feel different.'

'That's a good start. I'd like you to spend time with Tom and Thomas every day helping them to learn about each other and work together. Support Tom in helping Thomas so he doesn't lose his temper if he believes he is being provoked.'

Over the next few weeks Tom worked with the two characters and in the process learnt a great deal about himself. He stopped losing his temper and kept some of the characteristics of Thomas which blended in with his nature.

On his last visit he remarked, 'I still can't get over that first time I saw Tom and Thomas; it was a real surprise and at the same time I felt I already knew of their existence in some vague way.

The 'parts theory' is at the very basis of psychological therapy. It is a concept that is extremely useful in disentangling troubled minds.

By regarding ourselves as composed of 'parts' we are then able to view our actions from a different perspective. If I believe 'I am an angry man', this is very different from 'There is an angry part of me that takes over from time to time.'

This latter view allows me to distance myself from 'the angry part', to view it from a positive perspective, to learn about it and to change it, if I choose.

The parts theory helps us gain control of our actions and attitudes and improve them in a way that is suitable for our present situation. Often they are out of date, remnants of childhood behaviour that was once protective but is now destructive.

The following is a condensed version of a consultation I had with Annette.

'I need to give up smoking,' was her opening remark.

'Tell me about your smoking,' I replied.

'I started when I was 17. I've given it up a number of times but always go back to it. I'm fed up with being short of breath and constantly coughing. I make sure I don't smoke more than twenty cigarettes a day, but I must stop.'

'Why do you smoke?'

'I just love the feeling when I inhale; I also don't know what to do with my hands when I'm with a group. The cigarette gives me confidence. In fact, I don't think I have the confidence to give up.'

'It seems like there are two parts of you – one that wants to smoke and the other who wants to stop.'

'Yes, that's right.'

'The one that wants to smoke we could call the childlike part – she wants *immediate gratification* just like a child. The part that brought you here – the adult part – knows the damage smoking will do in the long run and wants the *delayed gratification* of being healthy.'

'I've never thought of it that way.'

'Let's extend the analogy a little further. Close your eyes and imagine the childlike part, the one driven by immediate gratification.'

'I can see her in the front of my head. She is small and says she wants fun and doesn't care about the outcome.'

'Now imagine the adult part.'

'She is on the right-hand side of my head and is very serious, a woman really. She is concerned about my health and also concerned I'll put on weight if I stop smoking.'

'Annette, it's a little like you are being run by two managing directors that have differing views and don't communicate with each other. Arrange for them to meet and negotiate about how the next week will be. Have them travel around your body – to your lungs, your nose and the excess fat to learn about the outcome of your smoking and eating. Have them negotiate an outcome that is the best for you.'

Annette sat quietly for five minutes, her eyes closed and an intent expression on her face.

'OK. They agree I will stop smoking. It will be difficult and the childlike part wants a reward for the hard work.'

'What kind of reward would be suitable?'

'I'll buy a new skirt at the end of the week – that will feel nice.'

'All right. I'd like you to stay with your eyes closed and imagine the next week with the two parts working in harmony. Notice how the lungs feel by this improvement in attitude.'

Again Annette sat silently with her eyes closed for a few minutes.

'That looks good – difficult but achievable.'

'All right. When you are ready, allow your eyes to open and make a commitment to spend time each day *re*viewing the previous 24 hours with the two parts and *pre*viewing the next day. I'll see you in a week's time.'

Annette returned the following week to report all had gone well and she'd realised the child and adult parts had been involved in many other aspects of her life. She had stopped smoking, had not overeaten and had bought herself a new skirt.

I wished her well for the future and advised her to keep up her daily communication with the two parts running her life.

Helping the players to be up-to-date enables the team to perform more coherently. Learning about our component parts, and coaching them from our present-day situation, improves strength and balance to cope with the ups and downs of daily life.

*If the errand boy is incompetent the whole business
may collapse.*

CONFIDENCE BOOSTERS

- Using the concept that you are made up of a number of parts, spend some time noting the character of these parts. Question yourself about the praiser, critic, worrier, optimist, catastrophiser, helper, fixer or acceptor.
- Are these parts helping you achieve what you want, or diverting you away from it?
- In order to increase your confidence would you make an adjustment to any of these parts.
- Choose a quiet time when you will not be interrupted, sit quietly and close your eyes, imagine some of the component parts that govern your life. Spend time having a 'meeting' with them in your mind so that you are improving internal communication. This exercise is very helpful in achieving harmony between the internal parts.
- Look at the role these parts play in your confidence or lack of it.

7

Confidence as Energy

One way to view confidence is to regard it as a battery deep in the body. Just like a car we may be complete in every way but our functions are minimised if the battery is flat.

We need energy to work our complex mind/body system. Energy to allow the heart to pump and the lungs to act as bellows. This energy is also needed for our moods, attitudes and activities.

When the energy is fully charged and flowing properly we are in a positive mood, feel we can achieve what we set out to do, are optimistic and 'feel good'.

As the power drops things change. We become unsure, our memory, concentration, sex drive and enthusiasm diminish. We lose confidence, focus on negative outcomes, and become depressed. Friends tell us we are 'not ourselves', we find it difficult to do things, fears creep in and we reduce our circle of activity.

Just like the car our performance decreases in every respect as the power falters.

I ask many of my clients where their battery is situated. At first they are confused by the question but on explanation generally point to their chest or abdomen.

'How do you know when the battery is charged?' I ask.

- 'I just know.'
- 'I feel happy and floating.'
- 'I have a warm glow in my chest and everything is all right with me and the world.'
- 'I feel tingly all over.'

And when I ask if the battery is flat:

- 'I have no energy.'
- 'I just can't do anything. I'm tired and irritable.'
- 'I fly off the handle, have a short fuse.'
- 'It's like when I have PMT. My husband knows to keep his distance.'
- 'I just want to be on my own.'

When I ask what helps to charge the battery?

- 'Getting a good score at golf.'
- 'Solving a problem, creating something.'
- 'A wonderful sunset or a sexy night with my girlfriend.'
- 'Receiving compliments.'

And what drains it?

- 'Being let down or criticised.'
- 'Not living up to my expectations.'
- 'Failing or being blamed.'
- 'Biorhythm. It just happens for no apparent reason.'
- 'Night time, especially if I can't sleep.'

Ask yourself a few questions.

If confidence is energy where would your battery be? How would you recharge it? What external or internal factors cause the battery to be drained? How could you minimise drainage of energy? Are the things that drain or charge your battery coming from you or from external factors like friends or situations? In other words can you maintain a high charge on your battery by yourself or are you reliant on others to do it for you?

The term 'codependent' describes those people who rely on others for their lifestyle. Such people gain energy from the behaviour of others and maintain that behaviour in spite of protesting against it.

The partners of alcoholics often behave in a manner that maintains and supports the alcoholics actions. This behaviour may be on an unconscious level and the partners only learn by discussions with groups such as Alcoholics Anonymous.

> Liza was depressive and anxious. She had a very good friend, Pauline, who was always available to help in times of crisis. As Liza improved and needed Pauline less, Pauline became angry and upset. She blamed Liza for many things and the friendship ended. Pauline needed to be a helper. She was dependent on Liza for her energy and when this dependence became less, she resorted to blame and guilt to deal with it.

When you look back on your upbringing do you believe your experiences charged or drained your battery? Are there any past experiences that are still draining you?

People with a high level of energy have the ability to cope with difficulties when they arise. They are able to rise above problems and find alternatives to deal with them. They feel a life-force that helps carry them through the day. A positive attitude and enthusiasm go hand in hand with a charged battery.

The opposite is also true. Low energy leads to a struggle to get through the day. Everything is a chore and the tendency to avoid things increases. People with low energy battle on two fronts – to cope with what life has to offer and the depressing feeling of having a waning life-force.

> Gail was a 35-year-old mother of three children aged 6, 4 and 2. She constantly felt down, dissatisfied and hard on herself. She believed it was more that just looking after the children that had caused this state.

PEOPLE WITH A HIGH LEVEL OF ENERGY HAVE THE ABILITY TO COPE WITH DIFFICULTIES WHEN THEY ARISE. LOW ENERGY LEADS TO A STRUGGLE TO GET THROUGH THE DAY.

She had many things to be pleased and proud about her life, but focused most of her attention on the failings and mistakes that she made.

When she was 16 she became pregnant and, owing to her parents influence, had a termination. She had never forgotten this or forgiven herself. She had a Catholic upbringing but stated she was never really religious. 'I shouldn't have done that,' she said quietly, tears running down her cheeks. 'It was murder. Seeing my lovely children, I feel the guilt even more, and a great sadness comes over me like a wave. I cannot help it. I don't want to be this way as I'm ruining the lives of my husband and children.'

I asked Gail about her battery. It was situated in her abdomen and was like a car battery, but it was old and battered – 'a battered battery', she said, 'just like myself'. It had not been looked after and she could decipher the word 'guilt' etched on the side.

'The battery was only half-charged and that is why I feel drained, tired and lacking in energy all the time.'

The things that charged her battery were the successes and adventures of her husband and children (not her own) and it was drained by the constant self-criticism, guilt and reminders day and night (in dreams) of her termination nineteen years previously.

Gail believed she should suffer for the rest of her life for her crime. She accepted the flat battery as punishment, but was made to feel more guilt by the unjust burden she felt she was giving her husband and children.

Gail's guilt was deeply imbedded. At first I made little progress in helping her let herself off the hook of guilt and self-punishment. I talked with her GP and he started her on a course of antidepressants. We asked her to discuss her guilt with a priest.

After a long time Gail came to terms with her guilt. She was able to put it in a more balanced perspective. She maintained her confidence and optimistic attitude after the antidepressants were finished. She chose to continue to see the priest and discuss other areas of her life. The process helped her to recharge her battery so that she could really enjoy her family and friends, and realise she was, after all, a worthy person.

The combination of support from her GP and myself, discussion with the priest, and the antidepressants, all recharged her battery enabling her to regain energy. She was able to continue with just the support of the priest and took on board the love and warmth from her family.

With time she was able to forgive herself and allow the guilt to drift into the past where it belonged.

In contrast to Gail was Steve.

Steve was a 50-year-old businessman who had drained his battery with overwork and was referred to me with 'burnout'.

Steve couldn't face going back to work. His GP had given him a sick certificate for two months and this time was running out. He was lethargic, tired, lacked confidence and didn't know what to do.

For many years he had been in charge of a firm in the city, taking responsibility, making decisions and under pressure for long periods of time.

His day started at 7 am and he didn't get home until after 9 pm. He never had time for lunch and if he wasn't at his desk working he was in high-powered meetings.

He described his condition as 'shell-shock'. 'It's like leaving the battlefield and not being able to return to the conflict. I couldn't face another board-meeting, another computer.'

As his whole life had been devoted to work he had not developed any hobbies, any contact with nature. He never relaxed: 'Don't know the meaning of the word. Always thought it was a waste of time – being lazy.'

We talked for a while about what hobbies may interest him.

'I once thought it would be nice to do some bird-watching – of the ornithological kind, I mean.'

I asked him to do two things:

- Listen to a relaxation tape twice a day.
- Find out more about bird-watching – societies, books, what you need, etc.

A few weeks later he returned saying he was a little better and enjoyed the relaxation tape. He had found out about a group that went bird-watching and was going to join them next weekend. He still couldn't face work but felt as if his battery was starting to recharge.

A few weeks after that he came to see me and said he'd decided to take early retirement. He knew he didn't want to go back to work, he had enough money from his savings and pension and was concerned his health would fail if he went back 'into battle'.

He was enjoying his bird-watching and his wife too had taken up the hobby. He was going to Canada for two weeks with the 'twitchers' and was starting to feel more at ease with himself. He was very relieved he'd made the decision to leave work and was sure it was the right one.

The last I heard from Steve was a postcard from Norway six months later. He and his wife were on a bird-watching expedition and he was feeling very well. The final words were 'my battery is completely recharged now and I don't intend to let it go flat again.'

Systems also have energy. Family, schools, relationships, communities have energy involved in the way they function (or dysfunction).

Being aware of this energy helps to make improvements if required. Often the system becomes bogged down and energy for motivation and action falls.

Recycling energy is a good way of maintaining a system, just as recycling paper and glass conserves the energy of many of the products we reuse.

In a family system it is possible to use praise, support and acceptance as an attitude to provide energy amongst the family members. When everyone in the family treats each other with respect and understanding, positive energy recirculates and enables each to reach their full potential.

Therese was a bright and optimistic woman of 30. She had an eight-year-old son Matt and had been married to her husband John for 12 years. He was a very different character – a real worrier.

'Everything is looked upon as if the worst is going to happen' Therese said. 'My concern is that it is affecting Matt, he is starting to develop his father's habits and I'd like to nip it in the bud. Is there anything I can do to lessen this negative energy that is circulating in the house?'

We discussed the family, the energy and the attitudes of Therese, John and Matt. I suggested John and Therese come together for the next week.

When they arrived John confirmed Therese's concern. He

agreed he was negative and said he had inherited it from his father. John, too, was concerned about the effect his behaviour would have on Matt.

We talked about praise, acceptance and optimism and how these could be brought into the family structure. I pointed out that Therese would be an excellent teacher as it came naturally to her to see things in a positive perspective.

I set them some homework involving John and Therese discussing the daily events from a perspective of positive and negative remarks. They were to keep a diary of comments and return in two weeks. At the next session John's opening remark was 'It's really difficult. I know logically what Therese is saying but I'm finding it so hard to put into practice.'

Therese remarked, 'I thought you did really well, I was much less tense than before and on a number of occasions you were much more positive than usual.'

The session was spent looking at different experiences in the home and how they affected John and what feelings occurred. Therese acted as a guide to lead John away from concern and criticism towards acceptance and praise.

I saw John and Therese every two weeks for three months. Things changed at home, John learnt to take off his dark glasses of negativity and see things in a similar way to Therese. The best outcome was the change in Matt which was remarked upon by friends and teachers. The positive energy circulating in the home was having a very nourishing effect and breaking the chain of influence started by his grandfather.

Experience is not what happens to you,
it is what you do with what happens to you.
ALDOUS HUXLEY

CONFIDENCE BOOSTERS

- Using the concept that confidence can be regarded as a battery, whereabouts in your body would your 'confidence battery' be situated?
- Is there a change during the day to the 'charge' of your confidence battery? Are there some situations when it feels really strong and others when it is not so strong?
- Often there are situations that drain our energy. These may occur regularly – giving a presentation, discussing a sensitive subject with your partner, saying 'no', or they may occur occasionally – asking the boss for a rise, being best man at a wedding.
- Think of what happens to your battery during those situations and focus on positive aspects of yourself that may reverse this action. Be aware of 'battery charging' aspects of your life – successes, praise, positive experiences – so you can bring these into your battery when it needs charging.

8

The Four Channels of Understanding

Any experience we have is channelled into four channels so we can make sense of it. We process information in four separate ways:

1. with pictures in our minds   –   visual channel
2. we talk to ourselves   –   auditory channel
3. we have feelings   –   emotional channel
4. we use movements   –   kinesthetic channel

There are also taste and smell that are important in specific situations.

When we receive information we 'go inside' and process this information in order to make sense of it.

As each of us is an individual and has our own personal history, our channel system, like our fingerprints, is unique to us. In the same situation we all react differently due to the differences in our four channels. No one has had a perfect upbringing, so these delicate channels have become distorted to either a major or minor degree. It is as if were are viewing the world reflected by a distorting mirror. We believe this reflection to be 'reality' and act accordingly.

We use these channels to know the world. We may use the

visual channel to respond to a situation and predict an outcome. If this picture is distorted so will our response be.

Accompanying this film and also on its own is a soundtrack telling us how to behave. This may well have been influenced by our parents or school teachers, so it too is distorted and may not be appropriate to the situation. We are also especially influenced by our feelings. Emotions such as fear, guilt, anger, etc., inform us about the situation. These too may be out of date and inappropriate and so not helpful in assessing the present-day situation. Let us look at the internal mechanisms of a hypothetical situation.

'What are you doing on the weekend, Jim?' Peter asked. Jim pauses for a few seconds, then replies, 'Oh, I'm playing golf with Fred. I hope it's a fine day as the course is really lush now and I want to lower my handicap.'

In order for Jim to make sense of the question he 'went inside', hence the few seconds pause. During this time he was seeing a picture of the golf course on a fine day, hearing sounds of the club hitting the ball and practising the movements of his golf swing. He may have been seeing the ball fall into the hole and have the good feeling of knowing he had lowered his handicap.

All these processes occur in milliseconds and utilise all the available channels. If Jim's visualising channel was not very free he may have focused on his feelings and self-talk to give his answer.

Because of past experience the channels may become blocked. We may not know why this occurs as it is beyond our memory.

I was giving a lecture on visualisation and a woman in the audience said, 'I'm a very good visualiser. I see things clearly in my imagination. Last year my son was killed in a car crash. Since then I am unable to form pictures in my mind.'

I assume her picture-making process closed down to help her by preventing her visualising the car accident which killed her son.

How does this channel theory relate to confidence? If we are trying to build our confidence through one channel and it is distorted, it may be helpful to switch channels to one that is functioning more appropriately.

If we have a critical voice in our auditory channel it may be helpful to focus on positive pictures in the mind to improve our confidence.

Two case histories clearly illustrate what I mean.

Louise had been abused as a child. As she grew she became disturbed in many ways and had difficulty coping with life. She had seen a therapist for many years. At one stage she had an intense desire to cut herself with a knife (self-mutilation). This is not uncommon when people have had a disturbed childhood.

Her therapist asked her what she believed may help prevent her cutting herself.

'If I had a tiger inside it would give me power.'

'Why don't you imagine a tiger inside then (visual channel)?'

'I can see a tiger, he's lovely but he keeps shrinking to a soft cuddly toy. He's not large enough to protect me.'

The therapist realised the visual channel was not working effectively for Louise. She asked her to demonstrate how she would cut herself. Louise made repeated movements in the air which struck the therapist as looking like a tiger raking its paw through the air.

She asked Louise to keep repeating this movement until a thought came into her head.

After a minute Louise exclaimed, 'It feels like a tiger. I can feel the power in the movement. It is like a tiger inside. I'm sure that will help prevent cutting myself.

Louise had moved from her ill-functioning visual channel to functioning movement channel which conveyed the power she needed to help her abstain from cutting herself.

I read an article in a fishing magazine by an angler called Len Colclough who kindly allowed me to repeat it here. It concerns 10-year-old Paul and Len who was helping a charity called the Second Chance which helps children who have had a tough time.

Paul was going on 11 when I met him. Pale and scrawny and a little small for his age but with darting eyes that seemed to take everything in without anything being registered behind them. I was asked to take him fishing for the very first time and to attempt to get to know him and to gain his trust. It was not going to be easy for Paul had a cruel history; Two years earlier, at the age of eight, he had suffered severe abuse and a beating that took him to within an inch of his life. He had not uttered a single word since that horrific night. Not one word to his mother, his teachers, the doctors, nor the caring workers who all tried to help. This was not going to be an easy day for me, I realised.

I talked to Paul all the way as I drove to the lake about everything that might interest a young lad: football, school, toffee, chocolate, television, girls, flying, getting egg on my face. Then I talked about fishing – still no response. We reached the lakeside and I got him to pay attention to how the rod was set up with the reel and line and hook attached – no trout in this lake, so I had come prepared with a box of wriggling maggots, two of which I managed to pose on the tiny hook while Paul watched fascinated (I think) by the non-stop antics of the bait. Then I dropped the line over the water and handed the rod to my disapproving young critic who had long ago realised I was just a 'fluff-chucker' and knew very little of the intricacies of coarse fishing.

A passing perch, several ounces in weight, passed by without a glance at the tasty offering and I realised that the bait was too high in the water. I got Paul to lower the rod tip a little and that did the trick for the next lazy perch found the ready meal at his level and promptly gobbled it up as his mother had taught him. 'Lift the rod!' I called. Paul did so and a bright, shiny, silvery acrobat of a fish shattered the water's surface and sent a shower of droplets into the air to glint like little rainbows in the sunshine. Then I was dumbfounded by what happened next . . .

'Hey, Mister, look at that! It's brilliant, brilliant that is! Look at it!' It was Paul's voice, excited beyond dreams, his first words for two years tumbling out of a laughing mouth and warming my heart as I showed him how to release the little fish safely and then catch another.

All the way home he kept on chattering away and I encouraged him with questions and then, as we neared his house on the council estate, I rehearsed with him in his first words for his mother. We knocked on the door and waited impatiently until her face appeared in the slowly widening gap.

'Hey, Mum, you should have seen the fish I caught. They were big and they fought and . . .' And on he went in his shrill little voice while his mother's face was a proverbial picture. While Paul tucked into his quickly prepared supper of bread and marmalade, the lady tried hard to express her feelings, thanking me time and time again, weeping and laughing at the same time.

'Don't thank me, my dear, it was the fish that did the trick by shattering that film across the surface and smashing through the curtain that was in Paul's mind,' I said in a matter of fact way, although I was bubbling inside, and as though it was all in a day's work for the volunteers who work unpaid for the Second Chance charity for children who need special help. And so it is, although my success with Paul was as enormous as it was instantaneous. That is what makes Paul my most memorable angler to date and I look forward to more like him in the future.

There were many factors why Paul spoke on that fishing trip. I believe one of these was switching him into the movement channel allowing a major shift to occur inside beyond his logical thinking.

The anorexic girl is an extreme example of distortion of the visual channel. Although she may be only six stone she sees herself as being fat. If asked to look in a mirror she will point out how fat she is and that she needs to lose weight. For a variety of psychological reasons her perception through the visual channel will not allow her to see herself as she really is.

Evidence of the movement channel is all around us. Being near an anxious person we become aware of their constant fidgeting – they cannot remain still. Their activity is directly related to their state of mind.

Calmer and more serene people have slower and more flowing movements to support their communication.

By altering movements – the way we move – we can improve aspects in other channels, hence the large number of people who *feel* better by doing exercise, going to the gym, jogging, etc. These people are focusing on activity (not thoughts or emotions), and by so doing are balancing the channels from feeling to movement.

Many forms of therapy involve movements to resolve problems – T'ai Chi, psychodrama, yoga, Alexander Technique, Feldenkrais therapy, etc. These activities are positive ways to utilise movements to balance excess or negative emotion.

The four channels of understanding are yet another thread in the tapestry of confidence. Having all four channels clear, working freely and in balance, enables us to achieve our potential.

Our confidence builds as we gain access to all of the channels and have them working in harmony, their messages reinforcing one other.

If one does not understand a person, one tends to regard him as a fool.

CARL JUNG

CONFIDENCE BOOSTERS

- In order to make sense of our experience we use pictures in our minds, talk to ourselves, have feelings and use movements. Spend a little time thinking about the role these components play in your life. Are you mainly a visual person or is an internal dialogue the main influence in your attitude?

- Focus on an emotive subject – a relationship, your children or some aspect of work. Think about which channel predominates to help you focus on that subject. Are you able to focus on the auditory channel if your dominant one is visual?
- In relationships there are often conflicts because one partner has a primary channel which differs from the other partner. For instance, the woman may be mainly visual while the man is auditory. The conflicts become apparent by the nature of discussions about contentious issues. Being aware of the different channels involved and labelling them as 'different' not 'wrong' enables a negotiation to take place rather than a blaming confrontation.
- Think about a relationship you have and explore the possibility that any differences may occur because each of you is focused on different channels.

9

The Many Levels of the Mind

The mind is a complex structure and may be viewed as being composed of many levels. Different levels influence us at different times. Sometimes it is necessary to explore deeper levels to understand the way we feel, act and behave.

Each level stores remnants of past experiences and we are affected when these come to the top (conscious) level and intrude on our logical behaviour. If we are in control of bringing these influences to conscious awareness they have much less effect on our attitudes.

Hidden Agenda

When something from a deeper level is influencing us but we are unaware of it, especially in discussion with others, this is called 'hidden agenda' – hidden from us but not from the person we are communicating with. We tend to use excuses and label them as reasons.

An excuse is an explanation offered for not fulfilling an obligation.
A reason is a logical conclusion from facts.

EACH LEVEL STORES REMNANTS OF PAST EXPERIENCES
AND WE ARE AFFECTED WHEN THESE COME TO THE
TOP (CONSCIOUS) LEVEL AND INTRUDE ON OUR
LOGICAL BEHAVIOUR ..

Nigel is a shy intelligent student. He is 20 years old and has never had a long-term relationship but is desperate to have one. His lack of confidence is acting on a deep level preventing him from asking a girl out in case he is rejected.

His friends have told him that a girl called Melanie is keen on him and he fancies her. He just cannot pick up the phone to ring her although he has spent a long time sitting next to the phone hoping he can pluck up the courage. As his hand goes towards the receiver feelings of panic and terror take over. He uses excuses as reasons both to himself and his friends.

The levels in Nigel's mind could be represented as:

Top Level 'I desperately want to ask Melanie out.'

Excuses (masked as reasons)

- She is not pretty
- I haven't got time

- I need to study
- She probably has a boyfriend

Lower Level The pain of rejection would be too great to bear.

Nigel may be aware of this structure but in many people the subconscious lower levels are beyond awareness; discussion occurs at the level of excuses masked as reasons. Until the lower belief is faced no improvement will occur.

Nigel and I discussed the effect of these levels and he gained courage enough to risk rejection. He rang Melanie and she *did* go out with him. The relationship only lasted two months but he gained confidence enough to ask someone else out. He *was* rejected by this girl but learnt he could survive.

Because of his experience, Nigel changed the lower level to 'Even if she doesn't wish to go out with me, that is not a rejection, it is a choice she has made and I can cope with that. It may be sad and painful but in time I will be all right and will have learnt from the experience.'

Triggers

When a trivial situation occurs resulting in an explosion of emotion it is likely that the system involved is one of a triggered response.

We pursue our daily activities mainly in the top (conscious) level of our mind. Messages from other levels constantly intrude as thoughts or feelings. If intense emotion is stored on a lower level from a previous experience, this may be triggered to shoot to the surface by an event similar to the initial one.

Being overcome by emotion for no apparent reason causes confusion, concern and embarrassment. Being aware that a 'trigger is at work' helps to make sense of the nonsense.

The trigger is a similarity between the initial emotional event and the present-day trivial event. This may involve any of the senses – sight, smell, taste, touch, hearing.

I had been seeing Tara for some months at my surgery and one day she consulted me at my home. When she rang the doorbell, I was in the garden picking a small sweet-smelling flower called Daphne, one of my favourites.

I opened the door holding the Daphne and greeted Tara with 'Good-morning, Tara. What a lovely day! Do you know what flower this is?'

Tara immediately burst into tears.

I asked her to sit down and discuss her outburst of tears.

'I have no idea what happened. When I saw you and you asked me about the flower I suddenly became extremely sad and upset and the tears welled up.'

'What do you think may have caused that feeling?'

'I really don't know. I felt perfectly well when I rang the doorbell.'

'Perhaps you could sit quietly for a few minutes with your eyes closed and allow any thoughts to drift into your mind. We may discover a few clues.'

Tara sat quietly with her eyes closed. Suddenly she said, 'I think I've got it. Gee, that's strange, I haven't thought of that for years.'

'What haven't you thought about?'

She opened her eyes. 'When I was little, about seven, I had a horrible teacher who was always picking on me. I was nervous about going to school. One day she came in holding a flower and said to the class, "Anyone who knows what this flower is put up your hand." Everyone in the class except another girl and myself put up their hands. "Come out one by one and whisper the answer in my ear." All the girls filed out and whispered the answer in the teacher's ear leaving myself and the other girl feeling terribly humiliated. "It's a primrose and everyone knew that except you two girls. Fancy not knowing what a primrose is. You are really hopeless." I felt terrible and wished I could disappear. I've never been able to look at a primrose since then. When you asked what flower you were holding, I suppose I immediately went back to that time.'

The similarity between the two situations was:

- Tara was unprepared for the question
- I was like a teacher to her – an authority figure

Asking her about the flower put her on the spot and she felt as dumb as the teacher had made her feel all those years ago.

The mechanism for a trigger is as follows:

1. A very emotional situation occurs in which you are unable to deal satisfactorily with the feeling.
2. The emotion is pushed to a lower level (repressed) 'out of sight, out of mind' and remains there.
3. A similar situation occurs much later and triggers off the dormant emotion, so that the response is out of proportion to the situation.

Using Tara's situation as an example:

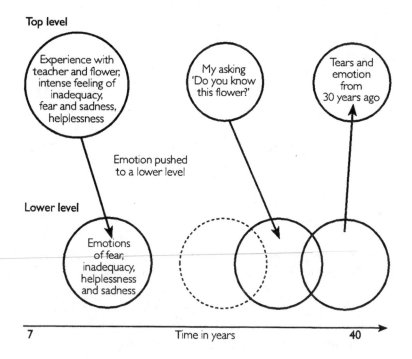

Top level

Experience with teacher and flower, intense feeling of inadequacy, fear and sadness, helplessness

My asking 'Do you know this flower?'

Tears and emotion from 30 years ago

Emotion pushed to a lower level

Lower level

Emotions of fear, inadequacy, helplessness and sadness

7   Time in years   40

You can become aware when a trigger is at work if the emotion is excessive for the experience.

Triggers and the Survival Mechanism

In order for triggers to work we need to have past experiences stored deep in our unconscious in a 'secret box' away from conscious intrusion.

These experiences are of a special variety related to survival. If something happened causing us to be terrified, humiliated, distraught with worry or loss of control, then our survival was threatened. This situation allows a protective mechanism to come into play and store that experience in such a way that we will be protected from a similar situation in the future. When the similar situation occurs the original experience is triggered and we feel just as we did then.

The protective survival mechanism works like this:

Life has its normal ups and downs.

Sometimes something *terrible* happens.

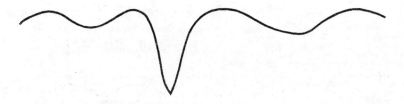

To prevent this happening again the lowest point of that experience is kept in a special box.

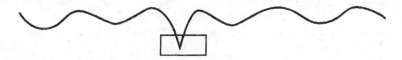

As life goes on we gather a number of these 'terrible' situations – being laughed at in class, failing an exam, being criticised by parents, getting lost, etc.

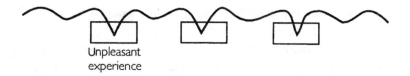

Unpleasant
experience

Each of these incidents is stored in a survival box protected from interference by our conscious minds.

When we have a 'trigger' in the present – something similar to a past 'terrible' experience – the unconscious does a scan of the survival boxes and alerts us to danger by reviewing all the 'terrible experiences' that have similar components to the present trigger. This results in us feeling terrible, panicking and dreading a catastrophe.

As we have actually survived the past experiences, and it is highly likely they are not relevant to the present one, it becomes obvious that the mechanism is not very effective. In fact it adds burdens to our journey. It is like a burglar alarm going off every time a leaf falls.

One way of dealing with this situation is to accept that terrible things in the past did occur, but remove them from their survival boxes. Go through the sequence of what happened and continue up the curve to a pleasant one. Store this time as a pleasant memory that feels good to recall, rather than a time when survival was in doubt.

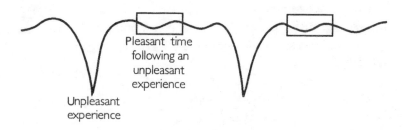

Pleasant time
following an
unpleasant
experience

Unpleasant
experience

When a trigger occurs and the review is done there are no boxes to review on that deep level as they are all stored higher up at a more acceptable level with the accompanying thoughts 'wasn't it wonderful it all turned out all right'.

The sequence is similar to going to a horror movie and being terrified. Then going back again and again until the terror changes into boredom. By reviewing past terrifying experiences from the safety of the present and storing the fact that we survived, we lighten the load on our journey.

Nadia hated being a passenger in a car. She would avoid it at all costs. She didn't drive herself so transport became a great difficulty in her life. Her husband had become concerned with all the complications caused by fear and asked their GP to refer her to me.

She recounted a number of experiences in her teens where she thought she would die in a car crash. In fact the car never crashed but there were a number of near misses.

One time was when her boyfriend was drunk, another when her father dozed off at the wheel momentarily.

These experiences were indelibly stored in her mind and kept in 'survival boxes'. Whenever she travelled as a passenger she gripped the seat, broke out in sweat, had palpitations and made everyone in the car nervous with her comments.

We discussed the concept of past baggage and I encouraged her to go through each experience as vividly as she could, making sure she arrived at a safe place after the near misses.

She became very upset as we did this, but as she repeated the experiences with the realisation she *had* survived, her fears diminished.

I asked her to repeat the exercise daily at home until the anxiety was replaced with boredom. After a number of weeks she was able to travel with her husband and remain calm and relaxed.

The graph of how Nadia's experiences were stored is as follows:

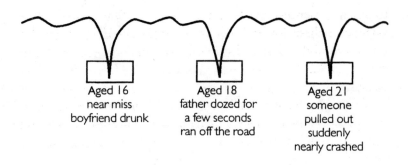

After she had reprogrammed herself they were stored:

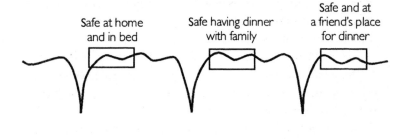

Reflexes

A reflex reaction has some similarities to a trigger. We react without control, a knee-jerk reaction to a situation.

Imagine I am standing behind a sheet of bullet-proof glass. I know nothing can break it. If someone on the other side throws a rock at me I will automatically duck.

Two conflicting messages are occurring at the same time.

1. My logical rational mind tells me I am safe.
2. The lower levels believe the glass will break and force me to duck.

The action of the lower levels is more powerful and overcomes the logical belief system.

Our confidence has a similar mechanism. We may know that a certain situation is safe but the messages from below (relating to past experiences) take over and cause fear. One way of reprogramming these lower levels is by *experiential learning*. If I stand behind the glass and someone continues to throw rocks at me, in time all the levels will realise it is safe and I will stand upright.

Building confidence, really means updating the lower levels. It is not easy as the messages from below are aimed at protecting you. The problem is that often they are out of date or misinformed.

Adam's early life was blighted by his aggressive father. His lower layers contained many memories where actions were followed by criticism. The message constantly playing was 'expressing feelings or opinions is dangerous'.

At the age of 40 Adam started to develop panic attacks for no apparent reason. He was fighting to overcome his internal critic and had been more positive over the last year but the panic attacks had set him back.

'Whatever I do I seem to lose,' he told me. 'If I fight the voice inside I get panic attacks. If I give in to it I sit around doing nothing and saying nothing.'

Using hypnosis we traced down a number of levels in Adam's mind. At one stage, he burst into tears.

'It's no use. I'm just no good. I can never get anything right.'

This was the level that needed repairing before Adam could gain peace of mind. The work we did helped him to realise 'I'm no good' was not a truthful helpful statement to have hidden in the depths of his mind.

He learnt to replace it with 'I'm a normal healthy man. I am entitled to my attitudes and beliefs and if I make mistakes I will learn from them.'

This process took many months as his father's criticism had held power for a long time. But when he left his panic attacks had disappeared and he felt better about himself.

Tracing down to lower levels we often find the statement, 'I am no good. I don't like myself.' From this root many weeds grow.

The message explains many of the restrictive beliefs held at other levels. If this statement remains, it acts as an unstable foundation to a building. No matter what you do to the upper structure problems may occur due to the lack of basic stability.

As the 'I'm no good' message has formed from negative brainwashing it is reasonable to assume that positive brainwashing will reverse the process. It is also reasonable to assume that it may take some time before improvement is noticed.

One way of altering this negative pattern is by 'affirmations'. These are small sayings repeated many times a day that respect, praise and accept you for who you are. These roots when deeply planted will grow beautiful flowers and bountiful fruit trees.

There are many books on affirmations (see Further Reading), it is important that you choose phrases that suit you. Some illustrations are:

- I am a normal healthy person.
- I am doing the best I can.
- I am sensitive, kind and caring.
- I am special; there is no one quite like me in the whole world.
- I will learn something new every day.
- Every day in every way, I'm getting better and better.

Affirmations have a certain format that enables them to be effective.

- They are said in the present tense.
- They are short and succinct.
- They are positive and only positive words are used (no double negatives to imply positive outcomes.)

The theory behind affirmations is that phrases repeated often will influence our unconscious mind. This is certainly true about our childhood where parental repetitions play a major role in how we view the world as adults.

Repeating positive affirmations can reverse the negativity of the tapes constantly playing in our minds.

It is not essential that you believe the words you say because it is only by repetitive listening to your own affirmations that you learn to believe them. In fact, if you believe them already they may be unnecessary.

For example, if you were constantly told you were stupid you may on one level believe this although the evidence may be the reverse. By repeatedly telling yourself 'I am intelligent', the phrases instilled previously will be replaced.

These affirmations can be dictated to a tape-recorder and played back daily. It is important that you give yourself time for this exercise and sit comfortably in a relaxed state to allow them to penetrate to the different levels.

Commercially produced tapes are also available providing affirmations on different subjects. There are also subliminal tapes where the affirmations are inaudible but drift down to the unconscious mind, although I do not believe that research has unequivocally proven the validity of these tapes so far.

Superstitions

For centuries superstition has played a major role in society. The Greeks believed their lives were ruled by the gods. If good fortune occurred they were pleased, calamities indicated their wrath.

In our society the attitude 'don't tempt fate' indicates that those beliefs still exist.

'How are you feeling, Mr Jones?'

'Very well, thank you – touch wood.'

Mr Jones may not be aware that the 'touch wood' ceremony originated with the Druids and their belief that oak trees were inhabited by the wood spirits. It would be very difficult for Mr Jones to refrain from touching wood as he believes this would tempt fate.

When I suggest to clients that it would help if they were more positive about the future they often reply, 'That would be tempting fate.' It is as if on some deep level there is the superstition 'If

I say to myself things will go well, this will incite the gods of fate to cause the reverse.'

This may well come from an upbringing that deplores boasting, arrogance or optimism and encourages negativity, self-effacement and humbleness.

Superstitions occupy a very deep level of our thinking, far from conscious reason at the top. They are very powerful and resist influence to reduce them.

One form of this superstitious thinking is 'If I worry about something, the actual worry will prevent it happening.'

Leonore's father died when she was young. Her mother had suffered ill health for many years and Leonore was terrified her mother would die.

For some years she had spent two to three hours a day worrying about her mother, constantly phoning and visiting her three times a week in the belief this would prevent her dying.

During the process of worrying about her mother Leonore neglected her children, husband and household duties. She was aware of this and it only added to her guilt.

At one level she was depressed and guilty about many things. At another level she believed the worrying would save her mother. At another level she could see this was all illogical.

Our aim in therapy was to connect all these levels and build her confidence in the process. The most difficult change was the superstitious thinking. Leonore kept repeating, 'What if I reduce my worrying and she dies?'

'Wouldn't it be better if you focused attention on yourself and learnt how this situation has come about?'

We spent many hours connecting the different levels. She learnt to share with her mother the superstitious thinking and was able to restore the balance so that peace was restored in her mind as well as in her household. Her mother *did not* die as she reduced the worrying.

The mind is such a multi-layered organ it is often difficult to discover the source of its messages.

Awareness is of great help in deciding how lower levels are affecting our attitudes and behaviour. Deeper levels often hide under the cloak of apparent reason. We need to be aware of this deception and discover if we are leading our lives or being led by past thoughts from below.

The only means of strengthening one's intellect is to make up one's mind about nothing – to let the mind be a thoroughfare for all thoughts, not a select party.

JOHN KEATS

CONFIDENCE BOOSTERS

- We often confuse excuses for reasons; we act on different levels to cope with both the external experience and the internal conflicts. Are you aware when you are using excuses and trying to fool yourself (and others) they are genuine reasons?
- External events – sights, sounds or smells – may trigger off a reaction in a deeper level of your mind. Your response may be excessive or difficult for your conscious wishes. Think of a time when this has happened and think about the emotions stored at different levels that may have been the cause of your response.
- One way of reducing emotions stored at deeper levels is to learn from experience, to focus on recent experiences that will update this feeling and replace it. Think of some experiences you have had that would dilute the feeling in the previous point.
- Our internal self-talk, occurring at a lower level of the mind, often has a self-assessment playing on the tape. 'I'm no good; I'm a success; I'm shy, etc.' What message are you giving about yourself from your constant internal self-talk?
- Affirmations are simple positive statements in the present about yourself. Create two or three affirmations that may be helpful and make a commitment to repeat them constantly to yourself throughout the day.

10

Mechanisms That Run (?Ruin) Our Lives

As I am lucky enough to observe many people and the way their minds work, I have learnt a great deal about methods used to cope with life.

Some of these methods are more successful than others. They all have benefits (the pay off) but some exact a high price for the outcome they achieve.

> I have such a mechanism that drives me. It is called 'keep the slate clean'. I have an imaginary slate in my mind and if anything is on it I feel the burden of that task that is yet to be completed.
>
> The benefit of this is that my 'in' tray is always empty. The cost is great because the mind doesn't differentiate between the value of what I have to do. If I have to buy a paper clip the concern is similar to if I have to prepare a lecture. I know there is something I need to do. This puts a strain on my daily life that is completely out of proportion and unnecessary.

Mechanisms develop as we grow up. We put instructions into the mind as a result of an experience. Once there they go beyond our control and run us instead of us using them as helpful aids.

A friend of mine described his main mechanism as 'When I'm on my death-bed I don't want to be saying, "I wish I had done that when I was younger." ' This meant he had to be doing things constantly in case he missed out on anything special. The words of his mechanism were constantly playing in his mind. If he was invited out or there was a circus in town he *had* to go.

When we talked he was in his fifties and he said, 'You know, Brian, all those years I've been rushing around doing things in case I missed out has not really worked. I've missed out on being with my children as they grew up. I am sure I will regret *that* on my death-bed.

We can start these mechanisms in the most innocuous way. My friend started his when he was 10. He went to see a magician who invited volunteers from the audience to go on stage. He dearly wanted to go but was too shy. That night he was really upset because he had 'missed out'; it was then that he formulated the mechanism that ran the next 40 years: 'I must never miss out on anything, I must take every opportunity to do exciting things.'

A woman who felt unfulfilled in life had the mechanism, 'I must worry about how others feel then I will be a good person and receive my reward in the next life.' Because she was constantly worried about others she was never looking after her own needs. Over the years her attitude was taking its toll and this was compounded by doubts creeping in about the existence of an afterlife.

Terry was 55 years old and complained his life was joyless. He had all the things he deserved but was very unhappy.

His method of dealing with life was to write two lists every morning. One list contained things he *had* to do, the other things he *would like* to do.

Because of his upbringing he had to complete the first list before he could start on the second. When he arrived home each night he still hadn't finished the first list, so he never did anything on the second list. No wonder he was miserable; he had a mechanism that excluded pleasure.

When we use mechanisms for one aspect of our lives we are often using them for many other aspects. I asked Terry how he ate his meal when he went to a restaurant.

'Oh. I look at the plate, see what I like most and leave it till last.'

'Is that a good idea? Does it work?'

'Not really. By the time I get to what I really like it is cold and I'm full.'

I asked him to go a restaurant and eat what he liked first. He took a lot of convincing as he was fixed in his ways. When he did go to the restaurant and alter his eating pattern, he returned looking a lot happier.

'I've thrown away my lists. I see now how ridiculous they were. I'm amazed I've been so silly for such a long time. I just didn't even think about it. My life is so much easier and happier.'

It's surprising how many people with psychological or psycho-somatic problems keep them a secret.

'I mustn't let anybody know about my problem. I'm so ashamed of it. It is my fault and I should be able to control it.'

If these people had tonsillitis or appendicitis, they would react quite differently. Why is something to do with the mind *our* fault and something to do with the body *not* our fault?

Panic attacks, insomnia, fear of the Tube or supermarkets, shyness, fear of public speaking, phobias are all problems that cause an immense amount of suffering. They are not the fault of the person who has them. There is no need to hide them in shame and guilt in case others think you are going mad.

In fact the more people that are told about the condition the better the person feels. It is like taking a load off your shoulders. For many of the clients who see me, their main task is to tell as many people as possible about what ails them. The conditions improve greatly just by doing this.

The sharing of hurt is the beginning of healing.

Louise was a secretary and she came to see me for help with a stammer. It was not very serious but troubled her and dimin-ished her confidence in many situations.

When I asked her what her friends thought about her stam-mer she replied with some concern.

'Oh. I'd never tell anybody I had a stammer.'

This seemed rather unusual as I assumed her friends would know by the way she spoke.

'I couldn't tell them, I'd be too upset. And what would they think of me. They'd probably think I was mentally defective.'

'But surely they know.'

'They may do but I could never tell them.'

Over a number of weeks I persuaded her to tell her best friend. It took a lot of persuading as she was very frightened of the outcome.

When she did tell her friend, who replied she already knew, she started to tell others. The more people she told the less she stammered. Eventually, it disappeared completely.

Janet had a problem being assertive. She attended many meetings for work and never said a word. She had great difficulties
with relationships and was as quiet as a mouse at any dinner-
party she attended.

'I have lots of things I'd like to say but I'm just too shy to
speak. I try and pluck up courage, get nervous and feel I'm
blushing so I keep quiet. I feel I'll make a fool of myself even
though a lot of things I would say, if I were confident enough,
would be very interesting.'

Janet was terrified of making a mistake. Terrified she would
be the centre of attention – in the limelight. As long ago as she
could remember she felt this way.

One thing she said which is a classical attitude of someone
who is frightened of making a mistake, was when she was eight
years old.

'I had to do an exam and when I read the questions I thought
it would be terrible if I got any wrong. So I didn't answer any
questions, I handed in a blank paper so I wouldn't make a mistake!'

Janet was right and also very wrong. By not answering any
questions she didn't make a mistake. But by not making a mistake she made the biggest mistake of all and failed the exam.
The aim of the exam paper was to see if she could pass not see
if she could not make a mistake.

Janet's life had followed the very course of her exam paper.
She had spent her life making sure she never made a mistake
and failed life in the process.

The work we needed to do over the many months ahead was
to alter her philosophy so she could change the rules that had
run her life so badly. Little by little she took risks to perform
tasks even if she made a mistake. From time to time she inten-
tionally made a mistake to learn it was not so bad and she
could survive.

She learnt to make comments and ask questions at meetings,
and in the process realised that others took little notice. She
talked a little about herself to others. She wrote a small article
for the newsletter at work.

Each time she actually did something we would discuss her feelings, how difficult it was, the reaction of others and the outcome.

We constantly referred to that exam paper when she was eight because she could see how limiting that attitude was for her life.

Some other mechanisms I have seen are:

- 'I must be in control at all times. If I'm not in control, something terrible will happen.'
- 'I mustn't grow up. If I do I'll be like my parents and that would be terrible. I'd also have to take responsibility and I'd hate that.'
- 'If I keep focusing on disasters that may happen, I'll be prepared for them and cope better.'
- 'My husband knows what's best for me. If I let him run my life everything will be fine.'
- 'I must rush around and do things quickly. I must fit a lot into my day then I'll feel good and be appreciated by others.'

In order to reinforce our beliefs we notice situations that support them. People terrified of flying will find a small article in a newspaper describing a plane crash in Korea, whereas those who are not phobic will miss the article completely.

It is as if our antennae are focused on receiving any fragments of information that will reinforce our beliefs.

Francis Bacon put it succinctly when he said: 'Men mark what they hit and never what they miss.'

The unconscious mind has a storehouse of fears and concerns. These are retained to prevent similar circumstances befalling us again. In order to protect us the unconscious develops a hypersensitivity to any situation which has a similarity to the original.

The protective mechanism involves triggers (see Chapter 9 The Many Levels Of the Mind) that connect a present situation to a past experience, creating emotion. The antennae of our minds are focused by these past experiences, causing an immediate and intense response when a similar situation occurs.

We all have mechanisms of one kind or another. Some are very helpful and achieve what we deserve in life. Others cause problems instead of creating solutions.

It is important to realise that once a mechanism is in place *it drives us* not vice versa. The choice we have is to alter the mechanism although if we are unaware that the mechanism *is running us* we have what I call 'an illusion of choices'. This illusion is a belief that we can change small things within the mechanism and these will solve our problems.

The real change we need to make is to *become aware* of the mechanism involved and improve, update or make it more suitable so that *real* change will occur and improvement will follow. However much one changes a train, if it is on the same track it will go in the same direction. Altering the layout of the tracks will provide completely new destinations.

A mechanism I like which comes from a sporting goods company is:

Just do it!

We all create defence mechanisms for our survival.
Some however, go a long way towards our destruction.

CONFIDENCE BOOSTERS

- A helpful concept is that a mechanism or belief influences the way we run our lives. Some of these mechanisms are useful, others are inherited or run by habit and are unproductive and harmful. Think about some of the rules you tell yourself and assess if they are helpful in running your life the way you wish. These rules are often brief sayings repeated in our heads, such as 'What will people think?' or 'I'd look a fool if I did that' or 'If I make a mistake it would be terrible'.

- Any faults or failings we have tend to be kept secret from others. Often when we share this secret we are pleasantly surprised at the positive and supportive response we receive. Think about a 'secret' you are keeping about your personal attitude. Do you think you would be confident enough to share it with someone close to you and learn from the experience?

Section Two

ASSESSING CONFIDENCE

11

The Checklist

In order to understand confidence it is helpful to write a checklist describing those who are confident and those who are not.

This is a general list – not a scientific document or dictionary definition. I have compiled it by recalling people who have come to see me and remembering their qualities. There is some exaggeration to highlight the points I wish to make.

Confident People

1. They believe in themselves, what they do, and that they are in control of their life.
2. They accept responsibility for their actions.
3. They are balanced in their attitude and outlook.
4. They have flexibility towards people and situations they encounter.
5. Their internal self-talk is positive, supporting and caring.
6. They aren't run by 'shoulds, musts and ought tos'.
7. They learn from their mistakes and see these experiences as helpful.
8. They are able to evaluate themselves realistically.
9. They can be assertive without being aggressive.

10. They speak calmly at a suitable rate.
11. They are 'straight' with their opinions and discussions.
12. They have nothing to hide about their personal beliefs.
13. Their body language conveys the self-confidence that they feel.
14. They don't need to be critical and judgemental to boost their ego.
15. They are good listeners and not overly concerned about what others think of them.
16. They accept themselves for who they are – neither successes nor failures.
17. When offered an opportunity they say 'Why not?' rather than 'Why?'
18. They see life as a series of challenges.
19. If asked what animal they represent they may say a powerful one like a horse or gorilla.
20. They accept change as a normal part of life.
21. They make eye-contact when speaking or listening to other people.
22. They call dealing with people 'negotiation'.
23. They believe they have the ability to influence situations.

Insecure People

1. Their body language indicates lack of confidence.
2. Their speech may be soft and mumbling or excessively loud.
3. They speak rapidly and with a nervous tone.
4. They need to override others' opinions to convince themselves (and hopefully others) that they are acceptable.
5. They are not good listeners and constantly interrupt to gain attention.
6. They need to be liked and fear rejection.
7. They need others for support and approval.
8. Guilt and fear of failure play a major role in their life.
9. They use *avoidance* as a major technique to prevent mistakes which they see as failure.

10. They are greatly concerned what others think of them.
11. They are worriers, and are frequently concerned about outcomes and criticism.
12. Their internal self-talk is full of doubts, criticism, fears and negative words.
13. They see life as a series of problems.
14. Their philosophy is 'Don't go in the race in case you lose.'
15. If asked what animal they relate to they would say a rabbit or mouse.
16. They have little belief in themselves as persons and undervalue and underestimate their abilities.
17. They compare themselves unfavourably with others.
18. They use questions as a major part of their conversation.
19. They expect criticism and often say 'sorry'.
20. They may have doubts about themselves, their abilities and others' opinions of them.
21. They misinterpret what is said in order to hear blame and criticism. This fits in with their internal self-talk.
22. They may use aggression as a form of self-defence.
23. They are shy and withdrawn in company and fear meeting new people.
24. They are scared of going to parties, being in the spotlight and making speeches or presentations.
25. They see an audience as 'the enemy' waiting to destroy them with criticism.
26. They feel safe with stability – any change is a problem.
27. Their eyes move around when they are in a conversation and look at anything except the person they are talking to.
28. They feel dealing with others is a 'confrontation' and believe that they will be the loser.
29. They are passive, believe they have no power or control and will be the victim of any interaction.
30. They have great difficulty in being vulnerable.

What Builds Confidence?

I did a survey of a number of my clients with a question: 'What things build your confidence?'

Some of the replies were:

- If I think I look good.
- Praise from others.
- Being well prepared for what I'm going to do.
- Being reassured things will be all right.
- Being with my friends.
- Achieving personal goals.
- Wearing bright colours.
- Someone, even a stranger in the street, smiling at me.
- Doing something I haven't dared to do in the past.
- Being less hard on myself, accepting I make mistakes and that is normal.
- To stand back and look at myself and think about what I'm going to do.
- Overcoming my fears.
- Having a go at more things.
- Spending time with people who are positive.
- Making decisions for myself.

Without self-confidence we are as babes in the cradle. And how can we generate this imponderable quality? By thinking that other people are inferior to oneself. By feeling that one has some innate superiority over other people.

VIRGINIA WOOLF

CONFIDENCE BOOSTERS

- Read the list of qualities related to confident people. Tick those you believe you possess and give yourself a score out of 23.
- Look at the qualities you don't believe you have and think about how you may gain these qualities using other chapters in the book.
- Read the list of qualities related to insecure people. Tick those you do *not* possess, give yourself a score out of 30.
- Note the qualities in this list you do have. Focus on just one of those and think how you could reduce it using other chapters in the book.

12

The Influence of Personalities

Our attitude plays a major role in the courage we have to face experiences. This attitude to 'those out there' is a mirror image of the way we view ourselves.

Let us create some hypothetical characters to illustrate extremes of behaviour. As we do so, assessment of their confidence will become apparent.

Victims

They believe they have no rights. Everyone else is more important than they are. They have spent so long responding to the needs of others they no longer know what they want.

Their lives are run by 'shoulds, musts, ought tos and can'ts'. They have no control of what happens to them and play a passive role to others' activity.

Worriers

There are two groups of worriers:

- Past worriers
- Future worriers

Past worriers are harassed by the phrase 'If only I hadn't . . .' which is constantly repeated on their internal tape, causing them to blame themselves for problems that befall them.

Having made mistakes in the past they are frightened of taking risks in the present. Their confidence is reduced in case the same happens again. Their head is pointed backwards instead of living in the present and facing the future.

The emotion that erodes their confidence is guilt and their password is caution.

Future worriers are never where life really is – in the present. They are always out there anticipating problems. Their greatest skill is predicting pitfalls that never occur.

They are run by 'what if . . .?' and see calamities at every turn. Risk-taking is foreign to their policy on life as it is fraught with too many dangers.

They are control freaks and plan everything to avoid potential pitfalls. They need to feel certain of any outcome, will book for the theatre a year in advance 'just in case'. Safety is essential and being less than certain is too painful to contemplate.

While eating the main course they will worry in case there is no dessert. During the dessert they worry in case the coffee will be cold. They are run by concern. Their confidence depends on the certainty of the future event. They make sure they are in control at all times and will not venture out of their safety circle.

Depressive People

They have run out of energy; their battery is flat; they 'can't be bothered'; they have lost enthusiasm.

Their main activity is to wait till someone makes a suggestion then negate it and tell you all the reasons why it won't work. Their main aim is to do nothing, as their energy level is so low

Their body language radiates the 'deadness' they feel inside. They have a major lack of self-confidence and believe that by doing nothing this may be kept hidden. Pessimism is their friend and ally.

Aggressive People

They believe that belligerence will achieve their aims for them. Whatever the question, aggressiveness is the answer. Their past experience has reinforced this attitude. They are insensitive to the feelings of others and are unaware of the difference between aggression and assertion.

They are very egocentric personalities, focusing almost entirely on their own needs. They are fixers and need to be in control, bullies who achieve things at the expense of others.

They have learnt that they can achieve results by screaming at people so that is just what they do. Any discussion pointing out alternative ways is regarded as weakness. They are very proud of their achievements and not slow to point them out to anyone who will listen.

Deep down they are generally insecure and angry. These feelings are often blocked off from themselves and if pointed out will be denied (generally with aggression). In order to gratify their needs they often surround themselves with victim personalities.

Shy People

They don't take control of their lives, allowing others to do so for them. They hope someone will fix their life.

Being assertive feels like being aggressive and that is the worst feeling in the world. Perhaps one of their parents was aggressive and they are doing everything in their power to prevent that happening to them.

They are 'waiters' – they wait for things to happen, but are unable to be active in achieving them. They have no power so need to be acceptors rather than fixers.

They know what they want but don't have the power to achieve it. Being quiet is what they do best. Their main aim is not to get in the way of others. They are run by their feelings and concerned about the feelings of others.

They undervalue their needs and overvalue the needs of others. Avoidance is the main way they cope with the world. They are always hopeful and realise the frustration of not being able to achieve their hopes by their own power.

Fixers

Fixers are focused on what they can do to change things or people. Any information received is channelled into 'What can I do to fix that?'

They are achievers and are 'task orientated' in that they translate everything into a task which is followed by 'How can I fix it?' Other people's feelings are not taken into account when an outcome is in sight. They are in their heads more than in their hearts.

They may be well intentioned and are often surprised when others exclaim that their feelings are hurt. They are symbolised by the boy scout who helps the lady across the street and is surprised when she exclaims she was waiting to meet a friend.

They are successful in their outcomes but have difficulties in their relationships. Often they try to 'fix' people and take others' burdens on their shoulders.

Their confidence is high as they are achievers and are focused on the achievements they can create and the problems they can solve.

Acceptors

They are the opposite of fixers. They are not at all bothered by outcomes. They are content to allow the winds of fortune blow them this way and that. They don't feel any need to fix anything. They 'roll with the blows' and are able to cope with any outcome.

They are not successful in a material sense but value emotions highly – both their own and others. They are able to find benefits from whatever happens and 'control' is not a word in their vocabulary.

Anxious People

They radiate electricity. When they walk into the room you know they are there. Their body language is that of fear. They sit on the edge of the seat, fidget, their eyes are always on the move.

They give the impression they are in imminent danger. They can't listen as they are focused on their fears. They may appear aggressive but this is a veneer acting as a defence mechanism. They are alert at all times, their internal alarm system constantly warning them of danger.

They have difficulty with decisions due to the influence of fear. They are constantly involved with their own needs, requiring reassurance at every turn.

Emotional Vampires

They are complicated personalities but you will know all about them if you have been in a relationship with them.

Their main ability is to find fault with everyone except themselves. Their main weapon is blame and they rely on the guilt of their victim to gain control. They are never wrong and so take a superior stance. They are good with words so it is difficult to put a point of view to them.

They are narcissistic, so are involved only with their own needs. They cause others to feel helpless and hopeless and are always right. They don't volunteer a suggestion but retort with a 'yes, but' when one is given.

They find change very threatening so do all in their power to prevent it. They have a rigid personality because of the need for certainty and control.

Deep down they are extremely insecure and have built up layers of aggressiveness to cover this. Their emotional reserves are at rock bottom so they drain the emotions of others in order to survive.

Enthusiasts

They are full of vigour towards anything they are involved in. They are super optimists and only focus on positive outcomes. They minimise hurdles and use their energy to find ways around them.

They are very keen that others share their enthusiasm. On an ocean voyage when some are lying in a deck chair with their pink gin, they will be rushing around trying to gather a team for deck-quoits.

Their focus is out there rather than internally. They are missionaries trying to convert others to share their joy in life.

They have difficulty understanding those that are depressed or pessimistic. They have the 'Let's have a go' attitude and their confidence is sky high.

They are great fun to be with and you are sure of having a good time. Perhaps they are easier to take in small doses than as full-time partners.

Confident People

They are balanced and have qualities relating to many of the characters we have discussed. They have things in perspective and are aware of feelings as well as tasks. They have an adult attitude and are able to be assertive without being aggressive.

They respect and accept themselves and know their limitations. They are also able to respect others and do not try to change them. They are balanced between fixers and acceptors. They have no need to show off their abilities and are always ready to listen and learn.

They are aware of their feelings and also the feelings of others and treat both with respect. Their confidence allows them to be open about their shortcomings. They are aware of their darker side and don't try to hide it.

All the characters I've portrayed are extreme and over drama- tised, to highlight some of the facets our personalities contain. We are all a mixture of different characteristics, a combination in different proportions. Generally one or two characteristics dominate our behaviour.

If you have identified with one or more categories check if you are happy to be that way. Perhaps find some categories that would suit you better. Note the components of these categories – what aspects you would like to achieve, then imagine how it would be if you act that way.

Maybe it would be suitable to accept the way you are and realise the benefits from that attitude. Note the successes and achievements you have gained from being this way.

Ask yourself if the underlying driving forces that dictate your character are out of date or appropriate. If they are out of date, substitute more suitable aspects to the way you view the world.

The aim is to have a balance of personality types so you main- tain your individuality and also have choices to achieve what you want in life.

Man who man would be,
must rule the empire of himself.
                    PERCY BYSSHE SHELLEY

CONFIDENCE BOOSTERS

- There are 11 hypothetical characters mentioned in this chapter: victim, worrier, depressive, aggressive, shy, fixer, acceptor, anxious, emotional vampire, enthusiast and confident. Considering your own personality, what characters do you possess? Are these char- acters creating a suitable attitude for you? Which ones would you like to change?

- Ask a close friend to read the chapter with you and have an open and frank discussion about the different personalities that each of you possess.
- Choose someone you know and check which characters make up their personality. Which of these could be improved to benefit the person concerned?

13

Coming Out From Behind the Label

If you go to an art gallery and observe the people you will notice many of them performing the following procedure.

They look at a painting for a little while, walk up to the painting, read the title and the artist's name, then return to their former position and look at it again.

Their second viewing is not through their own eyes; they see the painting differently because knowledge of the artist has coloured their perception. The painting has now been labelled and categorised, preventing them seeing it for themselves.

As Krishnamurti said, 'The day you teach the child the name of the bird, the child will never see the bird again.'

The problem with labels is that they are constricting and often inaccurate. When we label ourselves or others we are placing a limit on them.

If we were to say someone is a 'real worrier' that would describe one of their behaviour patterns only. There is obviously much more to them and this descriptive label does not include that.

When I was a medical student at a hospital in Melbourne I learnt about illness by examining patients in the various wards. Our tutor would tell us each morning what to see: 'Go and examine the swollen kidney in Ward 6.'

He didn't mention whether the person was male or female, old or young, happy or sad; all I knew was that a 'swollen kidney' resided in Ward 6.

Can you imagine how the person would have felt if they knew they were labelled as 'the swollen kidney in Ward 6'?

Since graduating from medical school I have acquired a number of labels – General Practitioner, Anaesthetist, Hypnotherapist, Counsellor, Psychotherapist. If someone asks me what I am and I reel that list off they would have disappeared in confusion before I'd finished.

I thought long and hard how I could reply to such a question and I thought about what I 'did' rather than a label describing me. I realise that what I do is 'challenge restrictive beliefs' and that is what I reply whenever I'm asked about my occupation.

The clothing industry has taken the labelling system to extreme proportions. Some years ago the label on a jumper was a small tag on the inside helping us to know if we had the jumper on the right way around. Now the brand-name is plastered in large letters on the front of the jumper on the outside. The industry has been smart enough to convince us it is fashionable to wear such clothing and advertise their brand in the process. These large labels serve to show the world we are smart enough, chic enough, rich enough and wise enough to buy the garment. The jumper does it all for us, we can safely hide behind the label without doing anything at all to promote ourselves.

So it is in life. We create labels for ourselves and then seek refuge behind them. We tell ourselves and imply to others we are a (insert label) and then we act accordingly.

Just as the viewer in the art gallery we need to know the label before we feel comfortable. We have great difficulty just being ourselves, requiring no label, just as the viewer would have difficulty restraining himself from checking the artist's name.

Imagine you give yourself the label of 'hopeless'. Your conversation would constantly draw attention to this fact. You would give examples to illustrate how hopeless you are and your life

IMAGINE YOU GIVE YOURSELF THE LABEL OF 'HOPELESS'... THE LABEL WE GIVE OURSELVES IS SIMILAR TO A JOB DESCRIPTION

would take on the character of someone who *is* hopeless. It is as if you have to perform in a play having the role of a hopeless person.

The label we give ourselves is similar to a job description. By constantly calling ourselves hopeless we work towards achieving just that. It is similar to a self-fulfilling prophecy.

In some way we need to categorise people in order to deal with them. Meeting someone for the first time at a party we ask questions to put them in a compartment so we can relate to them.

'What do you do?'

'Are you married, do you have children?' etc.

These labels we place on people help us to feel comfortable; we can put them in a compartment, we know who they are. A little like sound bites on TV describe an event. We know they are a lawyer, car salesman, secretary so that allows us to relate to the stereotype we have in our minds.

We give ourselves similar labels and our internal resources conform to the 'job-description' with which we confine ourselves.

If we use positive labels for ourselves this helps with energy and attitude. By giving ourselves the description – 'I'm a good person, I do the best I can, I take responsibility for my actions', we cope so much better with what happens to us than if we say, 'I always fail, it's my fault that things go wrong and I hope others don't find out.'

Jessica's label was 'I'm a born worrier'. She came to see me with symptoms of post-viral fatigue (ME syndrome).

She was a 30-year-old computer consultant. She'd had a three-year relationship with Tom and had her own flat in London.

For the past 12 months she had struggled to get to work. She was always tired and rested most of the weekend to conserve energy.

She had seen many doctors and had a multitude of tests and no specific diagnosis was made.

When I asked her about her worrying abilities she said, 'I've inherited that from my mother. She would have won a gold medal in the Worriers' Olympics. I'm very good too, anything that may go wrong starts me worrying.

Jessica's label described to her how she needed to behave. This constant loss of energy by worrying played a major role in her tiredness. She needed to find another perspective on life but this was difficult as she had totally absorbed the label of 'born worrier'.

It took months of therapy, analysis, reprogramming, meditation and affirmations for Jessica to realise there were other ways to see the world. At our last session she was able to say, 'I no longer call myself a "worrier". I am now an "acceptor" and it feels so much better. I'm able to allow life to take its course so much more than I used to; I accept mistakes and things happening differently to how I'd planned. I sleep so much better at night and I no longer dread the days ahead.'

Her energy revived too over the months of therapy as she changed labels and stopped constant energy drainage.

We are not a label. We are many many things and focusing on the positive aspects of our character is much more helpful than harping on those that need improving.

Perhaps when you next visit an art gallery, have the confidence to see the pictures through your own eyes without needing to refer to the artist's name for your peace of mind.

We can change the way we feel by changing the way we look at things, even if the situation remains the same.

CONFIDENCE BOOSTERS

- We use labels to identify a particular characteristic of a person. Think about some of the labels you use to describe yourself. Would you say you were happy, confident, relaxed, flexible or would you use labels such as shy, nervous, guilty, worried?
- As we often try and mould our character to fit in with the label we use, do you believe the labels you attribute to yourself *cause* your actions and attitudes?
- How would you like to describe yourself? Write down ways you could think, feel and act to fit into this description.

14

Change Feels Strange

I keep a beehive at the bottom of my garden. I get a great deal of pleasure (some honey and many stings) from my friends the bees.

They have amazing navigational properties – they use surrounding trees, the sun and other objects to recognise how to get back to the hive. They go out to collect pollen and nectar from the flowers and return in a 'bee-line' to the hive with unerring accuracy.

I cannot move my hive 10 yards from where it is. If I did so the bees would come back to the original site and fly round and round until they died. Even though the hive is only 10 yards away their navigational aids do not allow for such a massive change.

In order to move the hive 10 yards I would need to move it one foot per day to allow the bees to re-navigate to the amount of change. They can cope with that and survive.

So it is with humans. 'Change feels strange' and requires a gradual process for the transformation to occur. Part of you wishes to change – hence reading this book – part of you will resist change with every trick it can.

I have a theory that a very primitive part of our brain believes change is a threat to survival. It knows that at least you're alive where you are and there is no such guarantee if you change.

The part of the brain fighting any risk-taking is generally working with outdated information – relating to previous experiences. Its message is 'don't enter the race in case you lose' which makes sure you stay where you are wherever that may be. An improved motto is 'Better to have tried and failed than not to have tried at all', which supports the 'having-a-go' attitude. 'Why not?' is preferable to 'Why?' (see Chapter 21 Facing Our Fears).

The 'comfort of discomfort' is a feeling we all have when we've been there before. People who do make changes say they feel strange, confused, disoriented, unstable, frightened. These are normal healthy feelings – part of the process of moving from A to B.

I liken this to the feelings a trapeze artist must have. He is swinging on a bar high above the crowd. In order to catch the other bar he has to let go of the one he is holding. While flying through the air, I expect he has all the feelings described above, but it's the only way to get there. If he continues to hold on to his original bar he may feel safer but he'll lose his job and is unlikely to receive rapturous applause from the audience below.

Many of us develop a rigidity that prevents change. We become fixed in our beliefs and instead of using new information to change them we use it to reinforce the original attitude.

It is as if we have a theory about life and when evidence contradicts that theory we ignore it and restate our belief.

Isabel is a 40-year-old senior executive of a European airline. She had a terror of being sick or being with someone who may become sick. Her life was dominated by this fear. Every day, in the back of her mind, she worried in case sickness would occur in one form or another.

She would not fly in case she became airsick (even though she could have free flights anywhere in the world). She was married but wouldn't have any children in case she developed morning sickness. She would only dine in certain restaurants and eat certain foods.

Her problem started when she was a little girl. She was in school assembly at the age of seven and had food poisoning. She was sick over her tunic and that of the girl next to her. The girls around her laughed and teased her for some days afterwards.

She told herself, 'I would rather die than go through that again. I must never ever be sick.'

'Isabel,' I asked, 'you were seven when this very upsetting incident happened. How old are you know?'

'Forty.'

'How often have you been sick since the episode at school?'

'Never.'

'Well, as you haven't been sick for thirty-three years you must be feeling better about it.'

'Not at all, in fact exactly the opposite. I'm more frightened now as it is statistically more likely I will be sick as I haven't been sick for so long!'

Isabel's fear was so ingrained into her lifestyle, thinking and attitude that she interpreted any piece of evidence to reinforce her fears.

She saw me twice then failed to attend. Her condition was such a part of her that she had developed a fear of what life may be like without her fear. She was not prepared to take a risk. She may well have been saying to herself 'Better the devil you know that the one you don't.'

That Insidious Word 'Difficult'

Many people confuse excuses for reasons (see Chapter 9 The Many Levels of the Mind). They give an explanation as to why they cannot do something believing it to be a reason. Often there is no basis to it – it is really an excuse in disguise.

I commonly hear the phrase 'It is difficult' in this context. It is presented as a reason for not doing something.

At the end of each consultation, I generally suggest tasks to explore the theory we have discussed. These tasks are to be carried out during the following week and the client agrees to do them in order to learn from experience (the most powerful way to learn).

The next session is often like this.

'How did you get on with the things we discussed last week?'

'Well, I did try but they were difficult.'

'Difficult?'

'Yes, they were a bit difficult.'

'Did you expect them to be easy?'

'No, not exactly.'

'Well, what do you mean when you say "they were difficult"? I assume by "difficult" you mean you can't do them?'

'Well, not really. It's not that I *can't* do them, but I found them very hard to do.'

'All the learning you ever did was difficult. It was difficult learning to tie your shoe laces, to learn your six times tables, to ride a bike, but you did them.'

'Yes, but that was different.'

'Why was it different? If I'd asked you when you were learning your six times tables, I imagine you would have said they were too difficult.'

'Yes, I see what you mean.'

What is happening is that because change feels strange the client starts a mantra to convince himself he is unable to change. The mantra is 'It's too difficult' and implies 'Therefore I can't do it.'

For some strange reason, the anti-change mechanism of the mind grasps any straw to maintain the status quo. Telling yourself something is difficult is not telling yourself anything at all. We all know that much of life is difficult but that that doesn't prevent us doing it.

We follow the words we tell ourselves therefore by improving the words we will improve the direction we are heading.

Instead of saying to ourselves 'This will be difficult', alter the phrase to 'This is a challenge, I wonder how I'm going to respond to this challenge.' Another attitude is 'What can I learn from this experience?'

Both these phrases unblock the process that is caused by saying 'It's too difficult' which is associated with avoidance behaviour (see Chapter 10 Mechanisms That Run (?Ruin) Our Lives). By saying 'It is too difficult' we stay where we are, we don't take risks, we don't learn anything new and we don't expand our zone of comfort.

Being Institutionalised Limits Change

In Indonesia, some years ago, there were many political prisoners in jail. They had been there for 12 years. On the president's birthday, he granted an amnesty and a thousand prisoners were released. Within six months 600 had voluntarily returned to jail.

These people had become institutionalised. They had been in prison for so long it had become their home, their safe place. They couldn't cope with the change of living in the outside world with all the progress that had occurred during their time in jail.

We too become institutionalised in our habits, surroundings and situations. Although we don't consciously recognise it these forces are acting to prevent change.

Looking at the patterns we follow allows us to recognise the forces that are keeping us where we are. When we question things we take for granted we are opening some of the locks of our institution. Habit patterns don't like close scrutiny, it undermines their power, it frees us to choose.

The following joke is a great metaphor for our stubbornness to ignore the evidence if it conflicts with our views.

A woman was walking down the street and approached a man coming the other way. 'Why, John, I haven't seen you for years. My how you have changed. You've lost so much weight and you've changed your hair from black to blond.'

The man replied, 'I'm not John. I'm Peter.'

'Oh. And you've changed your name as well!'

The first step towards change is to change the word. Instead of using 'change' use 'improvement'. This makes a great difference to the internal mental mechanisms involved. It is less threatening, more positive and gives more incentive.

When you make the decision to go for improvement, remember the bees. Improving patterns, taking risks takes time. Slow increments allow adaptation within all the complex systems making up 'you'. Remember there are parts in there that require time and support for the process of improvement. Adapting to improvements will occur when you respect yourself and move a little at a time. Any journey, however long, only occurs one step at a time. Allow your navigational skills to become accustomed to the confusion that is an essential part of progress.

God grant me the serenity to accept things I cannot change,
Courage to change the things I can,
And the wisdom to know the difference.

ALCOHOLICS ANONYMOUS

CONFIDENCE BOOSTERS

- A comfort zone is the term used to describe our behaviour. It means there is a limit to the way we act which is caused by fear. Confident people have larger comfort zones than those that are less self-assured (see Chapter 21 Facing Our Fears). Some people need to sit near the aisle in the theatre as they are too nervous to ask if they can leave, others find it difficult to stand up to people of authority.

    Think about areas in your life where you are aware of the limits of your comfort zone. Do you use the word 'difficult' to maintain yourself inside your comfort zone?

- In order to move outside your comfort zone, it may feel uncomfortable, confusing or frightening. Is there any area in your life where you would be prepared to experience these feelings in order to expand your comfort zone? Make a commitment to put this into practice, including a time by which you will do it. Praise yourself for the effort you make irrespective of the outcome.

Section Three

CAUSES OF DIMINISHED CONFIDENCE

15

Knowing and 'Knowing?'

Some things we *really* know.

If I was asked, 'Is your name Brian?' I would say, 'Yes, I know it is.' I would be prepared to bet £1000 on that fact, backed by evidence of my birth certificate. I may be wrong and lose my money, because the certificate was forged or I was adopted, but my *feeling* would be that of *certainty*.

On the other hand, if I was asked where I spent Christmas when I was 16 (a *long* time ago), I might say I know, but this would be completely different knowledge to the one above. It would be more like 'I think I know' associated with lack of certainty, doubt.

Confidence is in the first category of knowledge. It is deep within us and does not have associated doubts.

We are controlled by three systems: conscious thoughts, unconscious influence, feelings.

Conscious Thoughts

Thoughts that are within our awareness can be said to be coming from the conscious part of our minds. They have logical, analytical qualities, make sense and seem to be in our control. 'I would like to go to the beach today' makes sense, is suitable and fits in with our attitudes and desires.

Unconscious Influence

An extreme example is the condition of obsessive compulsive disorder where the person is forced by thoughts beyond their control to perform repetitive actions.

The source of these thoughts is different from conscious desired ones; they are unwelcome and also appear to be coming from 'somewhere else' in the mind.

Less extreme examples come with phobias 'I know (conscious) it is stupid, but I think/feel (unconscious) the plane will crash if I travel on it.' Such thoughts are irritating and destructive and occur as if a computer has been programmed in the past and is continuing to follow the original program even though it may be out of date.

Feelings

These are a major factor in how we lead our lives. Generally they are more powerful and influence us more than thoughts.

They work on a completely different system from intellectual knowledge and if there is a discrepancy between the two, feelings generally win.

Feelings occur in different sites in the body – head, chest, abdomen and are interpreted by the mind to have a certain meaning.

Strong feelings are difficult to dismiss even though they lead us in a direction opposite to our wishes. They have a 'mind of their own' and reasons that evade the logical brain.

'I was doing so well on my diet, I'd lost a stone then I had this irresistible feeling to eat cream cakes and put all the weight back on again.'

When you 'know' something the three components are in harmony, agreement and unison. You know with the whole of you and no doubt or questions enter into it.

This is what confidence is all about. You may not be able to answer intellectual questions about why or how you know you are confident, but you know that you are, with your conscious thoughts, unconscious influence and feelings.

Les has been invited to stay with friends in the country for the weekend. He is confident about going and hopes he will have a good time. He knows some of the people who will be there and is looking forward to getting out of the city.

Theo has been invited to the same house for the weekend and is not confident about being there. His conscious thoughts tell him it will be great as he has been there before and had a wonderful time. However, his unconscious influence in the form of negative self-talk tells him about things that may go wrong and he has feelings of fear in the pit of his stomach.

Whereas the three components in Les are in harmony, there is conflict inside Theo which causes lack of confidence.

Additional information can change the 'knowing?' into knowing. It can affect one of the three components.

Theo may learn that a close friend is unexpectedly going for the weekend. This knowledge helps him to feel better as he knows the two of them will get on very well together. The feelings of fear in his stomach diminish and harmony occurs between the three components. In this way his confidence improves.

Unconscious influence can upset the harmony between the three components.

Giselle is 50, married with one child. She has a fear of going into supermarkets and has panicked on a number of occasions.

Giselle's mother was an anxious woman who had been hospitalised on three occasions for 'nervous breakdowns'. She had been on antidepressants since Giselle was little.

One of the messages Giselle received as she grew up was that the world was a dangerous place. This message still remained in her unconscious mind, although *consciously* she knew she was relatively safe with the life she lead.

At one stage in her therapy we used hypnosis, and when she was in a trance I asked her unconscious mind how old it thought Giselle was.

'I think she is seven,' came Giselle's unconscious voice from the trance.

Part of Giselle's unconscious mind had become arrested at seven years of age, a time when her mother was in hospital. For the next 43 years it was directing her as if she was a seven-year-old. No wonder she had a fear of going into supermarkets.

Our task was to help Giselle integrate her seven-year-old unconscious with her 50-year-old conscious. In this way we would be able to unite the three components so they acted as a 50-year-old.

The *feeling* component plays a major role in how we cope with the world. Emotions are very powerful and generally overrule logic and rational thought.

'I know mice are harmless (logic), but whenever I see one I panic, scream and rush out of the room (emotion).'

Many of our feelings are congruous, appropriate and up to date. They provide extra information. When feelings are inappropriate or incorrect they alter the harmony of the three components and reduce our confidence.

Some feelings give us *wrong* information. I call these 'phantom limb' feelings. People who have had a limb amputated sometimes feel pain in the limb that isn't there. They know they have no leg but the *feeling* tells them their leg is painful.

The majority of people seeking help in therapy do so because of difficulties with their *feelings*.

'Doctor, I feel depressed, anxious, guilty, frightened, angry, helpless, etc.'

Often these feelings have become exaggerated, distorted, inappropriate or out of date.

James had a fear that dominated his life which to most of us would be a trivial problem but to James it was a major one.

James was terrified of public speaking. The thought of it churned his stomach into knots. He avoided public speaking at all costs. He refused to be best-man at his friend's wedding. He didn't have a twenty-first birthday party and he made excuses to avoid his godchild's christening.

He knew logically it was ridiculous but his feelings dominated decisions on that subject.

In other areas of his life he coped very well, but there were a series of engagements looming in the next year and he wouldn't be able to avoid giving a speech.

Hence his visit to me.

James and I spent many months overcoming his fears. We used hypnosis, relaxation, speaking into a mirror, making tape-recordings, attending a public speaking course, exploring the feeling and putting it into perspective.

Eventually James was able to give his speeches. He didn't enjoy them and he was nervous but he realised he could do it and that he would be able to cope with any future speeches.

How do we achieve harmony between the three components – conscious thoughts, unconscious influence and feelings?

The first step is to be *aware* of which of these components is influencing you, be aware if you have the 'knowing' that means 'all of you believes' in your attitude.

If you are in a conflict, you will be aware that part of you is in disagreement with the rest, it will not *feel* right and you will notice hesitancy or lack of enthusiasm in what you are doing.

The actual effort of being aware of the three components starts the process of harmony. It is as if you are enabling a peace conference to occur between the three to decide what is most appropriate.

When you get the 'A Ha' feeling – 'I've never thought of that before' or 'I never saw it that way before', you know something has clicked into place and the three components are developing a similar perspective.

Being aware of your thoughts, unconscious influence and feelings is best obtained by having an open accepting attitude, not following repeated patterns and giving yourself quiet time to assess your attitudes in a non-judgemental fashion.

Listening to other people's opinions with an open mind also helps as it allows you to respect your own views and add new information to them.

Start by addressing one particular attitude you have to a certain subject. Ask yourself, 'What unconscious influences are involved, what thoughts do I have and how do I feel?' This will start the process of integration and balance within yourself.

When your conviction of a truth is not merely in your brain but in your being, you may vouch for its meaning.
SRI YUKTESWAR
INDIAN GURU

CONFIDENCE BOOSTERS

- Knowing about something is made up of three components:
  - conscious knowledge
  - unconscious influence
  - feelings

    Think about a subject you really feel you know and understand – perhaps a close friend or relative, perhaps some aspect of your work, perhaps a relationship. Assess what role the three components play in your knowledge.
- Choose something you are not sure about and analyse which of the three components is missing.
- Often we do things we don't want to do and put it down to habit or 'not thinking'. Check which of the three components listed above was playing the major role in that action. By doing this you learn to become aware of the influences on your attitude and behaviour.

- The most important influence on our behaviour is our emotions. As a rule they override thoughts and are often not amenable to reason. Think of some situation where you are influenced by emotions in a way that:
  - boosts your confidence
  - diminishes your confidence
- As emotions play a major role in our lives, think about:
  - appropriate emotions that are helping you achieve your aims and
  - inappropriate emotions that are diverting you away from your aims.

16

Misinformation

Our confidence is totally dependent on the information we receive and how we process it.

For most of the 24 hours of the day, we receive information from outside or from our unconscious minds. Dreams pass on information in symbolic form while we sleep.

Much of this information is incorrect and is called *misinformation*. It may be factually incorrect or just economical with the truth. Modern news coverage relies on 'sound bites', small morsels of information aimed at summarising the total picture. But this summary, due to its brevity, distorts the truth.

One piece of information that *is* accurate is that 'life isn't simple'. By reducing complex problems to a 30-second sound bite means we are receiving misinformation.

As children we receive messages from our parents by a variety of routes. Some of these we are aware of, others sneak in under our conscious guards. Body language, inference, modelling, subtle remarks, actions as well as the spoken word continually impinge on our learning process.

We cannot *not* learn from our parents. Our own beliefs are overruled by those of our parents, who may well be doing what they believe is best for us.

As confidence is built on information it follows we may have difficulties if we receive misinformation throughout our childhood.

A friend of mine bought a very smart Toyota car. It had all the accessories possible, even a TV set in the dashboard. As well as receiving the normal TV channels it had a computerised traffic indicator connected to a satellite.

This indicator pointed out where traffic jams were. The only trouble was that the satellite was still focused on Tokyo, so, as my friend drove around Knightsbridge, he could avoid any problems occurring in the heart of Tokyo!

This is similar to the misinformation we received in childhood. The information our parents give us may well be right for *them* but is not necessarily right for *us*. We often spend a lifetime discovering the difference.

THE INFORMATION OUR PARENTS GIVE US MAY WELL BE RIGHT FOR THEM BUT NOT FOR US. WE OFTEN SPEND A LOT OF TIME DISCOVERING THE DIFFERENCE.

I studied medicine before becoming a 'listener' to peoples' problems. The basic medical concept is that the patient is sick and the doctor fixes him. The counsellor acts as a guide to help the client learn about himself. Very different attitudes and I had to unlearn much of my medical training to become a counsellor.

In order to grow and gain confidence we need to unlearn those rules that are not appropriate for us. It may well be that these rules worked for our parents; it may be that they too inherited unsuitable rules from their parents. Whatever the case it is our responsibility to assess the information that we base our attitudes on and check if it is appropriate for us as an individual.

Role models, mainly our parents, have a major effect on our belief systems. At all levels of the mind we emulate the behaviour we observe even if we do not agree with it. A child believes that what happens in their house is the norm, they have no comparison till they grow older.

It is ironical, but unhappy parents whose lives are far from satisfactory, often imprint their values on their children. They constantly tell their children how to run their lives even though it is obvious they are in no position to advise.

Often we receive information we *know* is not suitable for us but we take it in because we have no protective mechanism.

Children of parents who continually fight are ingesting negative messages at all levels. It is unpleasant and frightening and the messages getting through influence them for years.

This ingested information is stored and acts as if the fighting parents live in the back of the mind. Internal self-talk will be similar to the words heard years ago. They criticise themselves just as their parents did.

To assess information we receive, either from others or our own internal advice, we need to ask ourselves three questions:

1. Is the information accurate?
2. Where is the informant 'coming from'?
3. Is the information relevant, appropriate and helpful in the present?

Looking at these three points:

Is The Information Accurate?

So often what we accept as accurate turns out to be factually incorrect. We carry with us so many pieces of information that do not stand the test of time. So many inaccurate facts are thrust upon us by newspapers, friends and ourselves that we do not have time to investigate them to check their validity.

Where is the Informant 'Coming From'?

If someone told you it would be a good idea to buy a Nissan car your reaction would be different if he was:

- a Nissan salesman.
- someone who owned a Nissan and wanted to sell it.
- a friend who had previously owned and liked a Nissan.

The information may be the same but our response varies depending 'where the person is coming from'. So it is with the information we receive from our parents or our unconscious mind. If our parents were alcoholics then we wouldn't respect the advice they gave while drunk. Questioning the part in our mind creating the self-talk enables us to find 'where it is coming from' and what value we give to its advice.

Julia had trouble skiing. She was terrified of the heights and chair lifts. Her family holidays were disturbed by her fears. When they went to the ski slopes either she stayed in the chalet or went skiing and was frightened all the time.

Julia's parents believed that pushing their children to do things was the best way to bring them up. She went skiing when she was young and didn't like it, but had no choice. Her skiing holidays were miserable affairs – trying to keep up with the others, falling over, being cold and crying a lot.

Some of these memories were still active in her mind and she received continual misinformation as soon as the holiday was booked.

Julia and I spent some time learning who in her mind was giving her frightening messages. She realised it was the child inside her who had such an unpleasant time on the slopes.

We discussed whether 'where she was coming from' was suitable for her present holidays and she realised it wasn't. She spent time adding new and more appropriate information at different levels in her mind, in order to build her courage. She made specific plans for the future holiday and was able to put them into practice. In effect Julia had replaced her infantile adviser with an adult one.

Is the Information Relevant, Appropriate and Helpful in the Present?

Often information we carry around *was* appropriate and is no longer appropriate. Attitudes, behaviour and beliefs in childhood *were* relevant to those times. Acting as children (many of us do) is no longer suitable in the adult world.

One major difference is that as adults we need to *take responsibility* for our actions and attitudes. This is much less so in childhood.

There is always an outcome to our attitudes and behaviour. As many outcomes are created by our internal information it is important to check that it is appropriate, helpful and up to date.

Lucy's marriage was failing. She was unhappy with her husband and his attitude towards her. He took her for granted and she felt life was passing her by even though they had only been married 18 months.

Discussing her attitudes and beliefs it became apparent that Lucy's marriage was based on misinformation. Her mother had been a slave to her father and continually gave Lucy the message – verbally and otherwise – that unless you looked after 'your man' at all times, he would leave.

Lucy had carried that dictum into her marriage with disastrous results. She allowed her husband to walk all over her and had no say in the running of the house.

During our sessions it became obvious to Lucy that the messages she was giving herself were not relevant, appropriate or helpful. She saw how they had affected her mother and yet had been continuing to follow them herself.

Over a period of time she put into practice attitudes and behaviour more suitable to her needs. It was not easy as her husband had started to settle into a pattern where Lucy did what she was told. He was not happy as she became more assertive, but there was enough strength in the marriage for them to stay together and form a new relationship.

It is important to check information that may influence your behaviour. Just because it is written down doesn't make it true. Much advertising is misinformation as is the advice we receive from every quarter.

I often hear conversations where one person is giving advice to another. This advice is already known to the receiver of the advice.

'Joan, you look really tired. I think you should stop work.'

Now, Joan already knows of the possibility of stopping work. It is not *new information*, so in my opinion it is of little value.

'I see you've decided to go to Italy instead of Greece; if I were you I would go to Greece, it is so much nicer.'

The person who made the decision to go to Italy already knew it was possible to go to Greece and for their own reasons decided to go to Italy. Offering a comment 'If I were you . . .' doesn't add a great deal because I am not you, and the person deciding to go to Italy has done so for reasons they alone know.

The piece of advice I have found helpful is 'Don't give advice unless you are adding new information.' This applies to relationships you have with others, with yourself and also for a counsellor/therapist.

It is difficult to give informed consent unless we are accurately informed.

CONFIDENCE BOOSTERS

- We receive information constantly. Some comes from outside – news, friends, books, etc. Other information is what we tell ourselves. Often the facts we receive are unsubstantiated and incorrect – misinformation. Think about some of the facts you receive and assess if they are accurate or not.
- It is important to note where the person who provides the information is coming from. For example, a politician may well be supporting party policy and is biasing the facts to support this.

  Thinking about facts and opinions you have received in the last 24 hours, focus on *who* provided those facts and whether this would influence the way you received the information.
- We constantly tell ourselves things – either about ourselves or others whom we know. We form conclusions from this dialogue which affect our attitude and behaviour. Think about some of the things you talk to yourself about and assess if the information is accurate or doesn't fall into the category 'misinformation', as it is either false or out of date.

17

I Just Can't Say 'No'

There is much publicity about censorship of four-letter words in the Press and TV. How much publicity is there for individuals who force themselves to censor a small two-letter word called 'No'?

Some people just can't say 'no'. In fact even the thought of saying 'no' gives them butterflies in the stomach. Their vocal cords do not know how to enunciate those two letters.

It's surprising how difficult it is for these people to say 'no', but it's not surprising how much difficulty arises as a result of this problem.

People who can't say 'no' lose control of their lives, they become victims at the mercy of requests from anyone who decides to ask a favour. Other people recognise this incapacity and make use of it.

'Victim Personality' is the name given to those people who are unable to say 'no'. They feel as if they have no power, are not worthwhile, don't want to upset anybody and, above all, need to be liked.

The sequence of events that causes this impediment may be:

1. Learning (incorrectly) they are not nice, of no value, unlikeable.

2. Developing such a low opinion of themselves they require love from others in order to survive.
3. Realising that saying 'no' runs the risk of not being liked.
4. Not being liked is the most terrible feeling of all.
5. Coming to the conclusion they must say 'yes' at all times.

Their lives are tossed and turned in every direction except the one of their choice. Like a boat without a rudder they are blown hither and thither by the wind of others' requests.

The ability to say 'yes' and 'no' provides the rudder necessary to direct our lives as we choose. It is a means of guidance through the rough waters of experience. Having only 'yes' at their disposal means they can move the rudder in just one direction – hence they go round in circles.

The bottom line with people who can't say 'no' is *that they need to be liked*. Low self-esteem deprives them of the energy they can give themselves so it is imperative they are liked by others.

The belief is that if they say 'yes' all the time people will like them and this is essential for survival. They go to extraordinary lengths to please others, often displeasing themselves in the process. The sad thing is that they are generally not much fun to be with as they have sold their character for the need to be liked. By trying to please everyone all the time, the end result is generally displeasing most people and not achieving the desired result.

The telephone is often the vehicle which causes problems. Someone rings to ask them to do something (they don't want to do) and they can't refuse. After agreeing, they hang up with a sigh consigning themselves to yet another unwanted detour on their paths through life.

A helpful hint about this problem is to brainwash yourself into having a parrot-like reply. This reply needs to come as a reflex, so it requires much repetition to replace the 'yes' tape continually playing in your head.

The replacement phrase is *'I'll let you know'*. This gives time, after hanging up, to gather strength and information and be able to ring back the next day forearmed with a reason why you are unable to comply with the request.

Other alternatives are 'I haven't got my diary on hand – *I'll let you know*' or 'I'll have to ask my wife and *I'll let you know*'.

It is necessary to recognise we are important for ourselves, we matter when it comes to decision-making, we need to put ourselves into the equation.

If I say 'yes' to you I may well be saying 'no' to myself and, as I am important to me, I'm negating myself.

> Sue really needed time to relax. She was tired and overworked but felt her partner David's needs were of more value than her own.
>
> 'Dave, I'd love to have a night in tonight, I'm so weary.'
>
> 'No, you don't, Sue. It will do you good to come out to dinner tonight.'
>
> 'But Dave, we've already been out three times this week.'
>
> 'You'll really enjoy this restaurant I've chosen.'
>
> 'I suppose so. Give me a little while to get ready.'
>
> By saying 'yes' to Dave, Sue was saying 'no' to herself. She was not giving the best to herself and therefore over a period of time would not be giving her best to Dave.
>
> It is important to put yourself first in order to negotiate quality time for others. By regarding yourself and your needs to be of value, you are then able to use this value in relationships with others.

Often the person who has difficulty being assertive is very sensitive to feelings – *the imagined feeling of others*. He is focused on the other person's needs and loses sight of his own. By saying 'yes' to them he is saying 'no' to himself. In fact, he is more important to himself than they are.

This might sound uncaring or egotistical but it is true. It is important to achieve a balance – one where we are thinking of the needs of others and also thinking of our own needs. To continually say 'no' to yourself is one sure way of reducing your confidence.

When requested to do something his internal self-talk is: 'She'll be very hurt if I say no. I'd better do it as it is *really* not too much trouble for me.'

The assumption that the other person will be hurt is not based on any factual evidence. It is based on extra sensitive antennae that are focused on other peoples' feelings, in the belief that other peoples' feelings are more important than mine. I can cope with the difficulties and they can't.

All this is pure hypothesis. Generally we never know how people feel unless they state it. We can use our intuition to guess and we can observe body language but if we ask we may not receive an accurate answer.

'Yes' people often become involved with others who recognise their deficiency. They link up with bullies who make use of their inability to say 'no'.

Patricia looked tired and dishevelled. She was always rushing, late for her appointments and never had time for herself.

She occasionally went to sleep during our sessions as it was the only time in the week devoted solely to herself.

She was married and had four children. Her husband was a businessman who entertained clients at home. Patricia was for-ever doing things for everyone else.

She came to see me for help with migraine headaches. After listening to her story, I asked her about time for herself.

She gave me a sad smile. 'I wish I could. There is so much to do with the children, and the home, and my husband. I'd love to sit down for a while and listen to music. I used to play the piano before I got married. Our piano has a layer of dust on it now.'

'Do you have any help in the house?' I queried.

'Yes, but they seem to be as much trouble as the children. I'm always looking after their needs too.'

'What about your husband?'

'He's lovely, but he's always so busy. And if he's not working he's out playing golf or drinking with his business friends.'

'Well, I think the headaches are trying to tell you something. Could you guess what that may be?'

Patricia stared into space for a while then burst into tears.

'I know what you're saying. I should stand up for myself more and stop being a doormat. But I just can't.'

She sobbed away for some time, then slowly dried her eyes.

'It's no good. I've tried to be assertive, say no, do what I want to do and it always goes wrong. I've told him I don't want to spend my life preparing food for his clients and he says we won't have any money if I don't. I don't know what to do. These headaches are driving me mad yet I can't seem to do anything about them.'

Over a number of sessions we discussed this terrible word 'no' and why it was so difficult for Patricia to say it.

We discussed her marriage, her relationship with her children, her friends and the home-help. We discussed her attitude towards herself and how she had learnt to have such a low opinion of herself.

She practised saying 'no' in minimal situations such as when shopping or denying some of the children's more expensive demands.

It was very difficult for her but she saw it as the only way to improve her lifestyle. She was able to have time for herself, and refuse some requests. She did make improvements that allowed her to turn the rudder of her life in more than one direction.

It is interesting that the other side of the *same* coin are those who say 'no' all the time. These people also lack confidence and use 'no' as a protective barrier to defend their fortress of shyness.

These people use 'no' to avoid change – change is seen as threatening, a chance for failure. Failure is the worst thing that can happen as it highlights their basic inadequacy. Problems arise because saying 'no' to risks is saying 'no' to life. Staying behind the protective barricade of 'no' means they are unable to interact with others, make mistakes, learn.

For these people any words that will prevent intrusion and maintain the status quo are used. Phrases such as 'yes, but', 'I'm sorry, I can't', 'I'll think about it', 'I would, but' are all rehearsed at the first suggestion of doing something new. They feel safe inside their barricade and unsafe venturing into the world of exploring, taking risks or 'having a go'.

Saying 'no' to others may well mean you are saying 'yes' to yourself.

CONFIDENCE BOOSTERS

- For people who cannot say 'no' life is very difficult. Are you one of those people? Do you use any means possible to avoid saying 'no' and has this caused problems?

  Think of phrases you may use such as, 'I'll let you know', 'I'm not sure just now', 'I'd prefer not to at present' – that will give you breathing space and help you avoid saying 'yes' every time.

- Realise that you *are* of value so your needs are taken into consideration whenever you are discussing options with someone. By stating your needs it is possible to negotiate an outcome that is favourable to both.

- It is possible to reprogram the neural pathways in your mind by constant repetition. By repeatedly saying 'no' out loud when you are on your own you are starting to change these pathways and make it a more familiar word so it can be used when appropriate.

18

Pressure From Without and Within

One of the most common complaints I hear is, 'I can't cope with the pressure.'

The word 'pressure' may relate to work, home life, not enough money, expectations from others, too many things to do, etc.

A concept which I have found very helpful is that of 'the internal and external masters'.

We are mainly driven by two forces:

- The requirements coming from within – the needs of our body, mind and soul.
- The external requirements – work, having enough money to pay the rent, children's needs, partner's demands, etc.

Often we are out of balance. We pay too much heed to the external master and neglect the internal one. This causes problems with ill health and lack of energy. These conditions compound the problem as they put more pressure on our daily routine of coping with life.

I believe it is important to recognise our internal master. It is less vocal and its needs are less obvious than the external one. It is often crying out for help but we do not hear it or heed it.

Deborah was 20. She was studying for law exams and was just staring into space, unable to take in any information from her law books.

She looked exhausted and very worried.

'If I don't pass I'm in big trouble. It is essential I get good grades so I can practice law like my father. He's promised I can do my article clerk term in his office.'

Deborah had been a bright vivacious girl who loved sport and had many friends. Over the last year she had closeted herself with her books and studied night and day. She had neglected her inner needs – the internal mistress – and focused on the external need to pass the law exam so she could work with her father.

Over the past year she had become out of balance and her mind was telling her so. It was saying 'I can take no more' and it was doing so in a most appropriate way.

Deborah needed to rest from her books and go into a passive fallow time allowing her body to build up energy again. The pressure she was exerting on herself was just too much for her mind and body to handle.

There was six months till the exams and I told her she needed three weeks completely away from the books. She was aghast at the thought and said she couldn't possibly do that.

I pointed out that if she continued doing what she was doing, not only would she fail the exams but she may also become ill. We argued for some time and came to a compromise that for the next week she would only work in the mornings and have the afternoons completely out of the house and away from her books.

When I saw her the following week, she looked a little better but very worried.

'I can't do it, doctor. I spend all the afternoon worrying about the work I have to do to catch up. I go out but I'm not really there. I'm having trouble sleeping because I'm so worried.'

We then discussed a timetable for her work and leisure. A framework that would help her see she would cover the work and also be able to have time off. A lawyer friend of hers agreed to supervise the program and that seemed to do the trick.

She followed a regimented pattern of work and relaxation supervised by her friend and myself and did in fact survive the six months and pass her exams. Respecting the need for client confidentiality I asked Deborah if I could speak to her father. She agreed and I suggested to him that Deborah have a long relaxing holiday before starting her article year.

Deborah was putting great pressure on herself. The pressure was compounded by the need to show her father she could do it.

People don't realise it is generally themselves who are responsible for the pressure they feel. There may be external factors but these are translated into 'self-pressure' in order to achieve, be successful, gain respect, etc.

For some, pressure boosts confidence and provides the stimulus to achieve their full potential. For others it has the reverse effect.

A seamstress was renowned for the rapidity and excellence of her work. She threaded the needle automatically and sewed beautiful garments.

She was invited to display her talents on TV. Under the glare of the lights, the focus of the cameras and the presence of the audience, she could not even thread the needle.

She suffered from 'performance anxiety'. No wonder! The peace of her home was in stark contrast to the pressure of the TV studio.

Performance anxiety is seen in many areas of life. The pressure we put on ourselves to perform is so great it has the completely opposite effect. It occurs in speeches, presentations, sex, work, sport, exams, in fact in any activity where the outcome is very important.

We start an internal tape: 'I've got to do it. If I fail the outcome will be terrible.'

The pressure affects the system – whichever one is involved – making it much more difficult to perform.

I repeat *the pressure comes from within us*: we may say 'they are making me' but in reality we are *making ourselves* by the musts, shoulds and ought to's.

Another major pressure is *the pressure of time*. Our life is run by the clock. Time to get up, deadlines, time to get to work, time to get the kids from school, time to cook the dinner, etc. It is as if some invisible person is holding a clock and pointing at us saying, 'Watch the time, you're going to be late.' We feel as if we are going as fast as we can, but being on a treadmill we are going nowhere.

Time is a basic concept of nature. Squirrels who do not own a Rolex still feel the pressure to gather the nuts before winter sets in. Birds, unaware of the meaning of a minute, know when to fly south to avoid the impending cold. They too must feel time pressure as a survival mechanism.

How often do we look at our watches to check where we are in relation to time? It is like a ship's captain constantly checking the compass to get his bearings.

Many of us need to 'touch base' with the clock to see if we are on course for the program we set ourselves at the start of the day. Even when we are not looking at our watch our minds are alert to the passing of time.

A number of people have sought help because their internal clocks are out of sync with Greenwich Mean Time.

Some say they *have* to be early, others are *always* late. This mistiming causes problems in relationships and increases the pressure of time. Their internal clocks are either fast or slow telling them to hurry or dawdle with resulting difficulties.

Logic and experience have little effect in adjusting these internal time pieces, in spite of all the angry hostesses, missed shows, irate partners, their clocks still dictate their behaviour.

I have found a useful concept to deal with this difficulty with time, I call it the *internal metronome*.

Imagine a metronome inside you like the conductor of an orchestra. You have a natural rate that is comfortable for you. It may be different from others around you and may alter with different situations. If you are sitting relaxed in a chair this metronome would go at a rate that would allow all the systems in your body – heart, lungs, kidneys, brain – to work at their best.

When clients see me I ask them to sit in the chair with their eyes closed. I play an actual metronome and they tell me to go faster or slower till it reaches a comfortable rate for them.

Difficulties arise when outside pressures direct you to go faster than your natural rate. Your partner may have a faster metronome than you do. She may be constantly saying 'hurry up' implying you are slow. This pressure has its effect and arguments follow.

The deadlines at work may require a rate of 150 per minute and you are comfortable with 50 per minute. It is easy to see where stress and symptoms occur after prolonged periods at 150 per minute.

Mary had physical problems. She couldn't swallow. The doctors had done many tests which were all normal. They suggested there may be a psychological component and she was referred to me.

Mary's mother had been very successful. She ran a number of charities and was constantly doing things in a very efficient way. Mary was trying to keep up with her mother and had a terror of 'being too slow'. She tried to fit too much into her day and felt guilty if she failed.

I asked her to sit with her eyes closed and listen to the metronome until it was at a comfortable rate.

Her natural rate was 56 beats per minute. 'That feels wonderful' she said. 'It's so calm and tranquil I could go to sleep.'

I then asked her to tell me what rate she ran her daily life. I increased the speed of the metronome till we got to 200 beats per minute.

'That's about right. That's how I go from morning till night.'

'Why do you do that?'

'Otherwise I'd never get everything done.'

Mary's symptoms were, in my opinion, due to the fact she was putting herself under the time pressure of 200 beats per minute when her natural rate was 56. Her body just 'couldn't swallow' the demands she was putting on herself.

The complex commodity called confidence is intertwined among this process of pressure. In Mary's case she did not have the confidence to be herself, she had to emulate her mother.

Pressure from without is transformed into pressure from within. With confidence we have some control in this transformation and can protect ourselves from outside influence. We do not need to be at the mercy of the timing of others.

I understand that many times we need to conform to the time pressures of some situations. If that is so, it is important to restore the balance with time for yourself, time to go at your own rate, time to respect your internal master.

Stress is the fear of losing control.

CONFIDENCE BOOSTERS

- Pressure can be exerted on ourselves from within or without. We tell ourselves we must, should, ought to do things creating a pressure to do so. Thinking about how pressure affects your life, note what proportion is owing to outside influence and what proportion created by your own self-talk.

- One component of pressure is related to time. Are you someone who is constantly aware of the clock or do you get things done in your own time?

- There is a concept that we have an internal timing device that is specific for ourselves. Are you aware whether your internal metronome is going fast or slow? How does your rate compare with your partner's? Is your rate suitable for your lifestyle and peace of mind or does it cause time pressure and tension?

Section Four

Ways To Improve Confidence

19

Self-Help Techniques

There are many ways we can help ourselves cope with life. Every day presents us with experiences that require decisions. By learning techniques that will make those decisions easier we will build confidence for the next day.

Self-Praise

Having a positive attitude to ourselves. This attitude provides internal support and confidence in whatever we do.

'Well done.' 'You can do it.' 'Remember when you succeeded before.'

This attitude is such a contrast to the words we constantly hear from the less confident.

'I'm hopeless.' 'I know it won't work.' 'Why does it always happen to me?'

These sayings came about from early learning. An experiment with seven-year-old children in America, where a tape-recorder was strapped to them for 24 hours to record what they heard, showed that 75 per cent of the comments they received from adults was negative.

'Don't do this.' 'You mustn't say that.' 'You are just no good.'

This brainwashing caused negative self-talk to continue in the brain long after the adults had stopped. These children learnt how to criticise themselves and were taught that self-praise was boastful and egotistical.

Nuisances or Problems

A problem is defined as 'anything, matter or person that is difficult to deal with'. If we have a problem we spend time and energy looking for a solution. Many people regard the majority of things in their life as 'problems'. Such a person is constantly focused on the 'problem' and misses out on the good things in their lives.

A nuisance is defined as a 'person or thing that causes annoyance' – no mention of problem or seeking a solution.

We approach nuisances with a completely different attitude to problems. We accept them; we don't like them but we put up with them as they may be unchangeable. They may not be worth the effort of trying to 'fix' them.

I was waiting at the bus-stop one day and the bus was late. This is not an unusual phenomenon. The man in the queue next to me was getting agitated. He kept looking at his watch and looking down the street. He muttered to himself about the 'problem of buses being late'.

All his muttering was not going 'to solve the problem' and create a bus over the horizon. It was a nuisance and it may have made him late for an appointment, but by labelling it as a problem, he was automatically trying to find a solution.

My suggestion is to check how many so-called problems weighing down your daily activities can be relabelled as nuisances and accepted as such. This lightens the load and allows things to flow more smoothly with less resistance.

When you are worrying about something, trying to fix it, ask yourself if it is a problem or a nuisance. Is it something that is devastating or just irritating? If you put up with it, will it resolve with time or does it need your time and energy to resolve it?

A saying that I find very helpful is: *Whatever it is that causes concern today – one day it will be just a memory.*

It is also possible to respond to problems as challenges or opportunities for learning. If you ask yourself 'What can I learn from this?' you will be starting a completely different and rewarding mechanism in the mind than if you say 'This is a problem, why does it always happen to me?'

Future Worriers

If we anticipate problems ahead we will worry about what may happen. Most times what may happen doesn't happen and all the worry energy goes down the drain – no use at all.

Some people are involved in 'superstitious thinking' (see Chapter 9 The Many Levels of the Mind). They believe that their worry actually prevents disaster. There is some mysterious power that causes catastrophes unless they worry about them. Once they stop worrying their protection is lost and disaster will strike.

Worry does have a negative effect. It focuses on the problem not the solution, blinkers us from good things that lie ahead, causes fear and drains confidence.

Possibility and probability

A technique to help worriers is to differentiate between possibilities and probabilities. I have found this technique to be very helpful.

Sit quietly with your eyes closed and imagine a very small container the size of a thimble on the left side of your mind. Label it 'Possibility'. On the right side see a large container, the size of a house, labelled 'Probability'.

A TECHNIQUE TO HELP WORRIERS IS TO DIFFERENTIATE BETWEEN *PROBABILITIES* AND *POSSIBILITIES* . . .

We lead our lives according to the probability of what may happen. If you go down the street to buy a newspaper the probability is that you will do just that. The possibilities are that you will be mugged, a brick may fall on your head or you will be run over by a car, but these are possibilities and you give them minimal attention.

Fear causes possibilities to jump out of the thimble sized container into the large one and be treated as probabilities. This causes future worrying as you then have an inaccurate perspective on life. Imagine going to get a paper and focusing most of your attention on whether you would be mugged or not!

The aim is to put those possibilities back into the thimble where they belong giving them the appropriate amount of attention. You can't say they definitely won't happen, but you only give them a minute amount of concern. This allows you to restore the balance so your attention will be focused on the probabilities.

Practising this technique every day allows the occupants of the two containers to be helpful and appropriate.

Acceptance of Self or Fear of Rejection

As we grew up we required a number of supporting influences to provide a trellis, a framework to allow us to build self-confidence. This framework is composed of many elements (see Chapter 30 Helping Your Children Become Confident) including love, support, recognition for who we were as individuals, understanding, acceptance and praise.

Trust is an important commodity which binds all these factors. We need to trust our parents in order to send out the delicate shoots of learning and confidence. It is a slow step-by-step process requiring patience and care.

If we are supported, praised, encouraged and recognised for who we are then we proceed far more smoothly up the trellis of childhood.

However, if we feel rejected the pain causes an abrupt cessation of growth. We store this pain in our memory bank and make unconscious decisions to avoid it in future.

To protect us from the pain of rejection we build a wall. Walls have the advantage of keeping nasty things out but at the same time they prevent us sharing ourselves with the outside world. By retreating into ourselves for protection we do not have experiences necessary for confidence building.

This fear of rejection inevitably colours many situations from deep and meaningful relationships to giving a wedding speech as best-man.

The opposite to this fear is the ability to be *vulnerable*. This is a process of lowering walls and allowing others to know you as you really are, warts and all. It involves overcoming fears, liking yourself and taking risks to trust others with your sensitive self.

We gain strength as we grow and our powers are greater than when we were children. Learning to trust these powers of dealing with adversity, helps us lower the walls and show our vulnerability. Confidence grows hand in hand as we reduce the fear of rejection, remove the protective walls and build the freedom to be vulnerable.

Knowledge comes, but wisdom lingers.
ALFRED LORD TENNYSON

CONFIDENCE BOOSTERS

- Things that trouble us can be described as problems or nuisances. Problems cause us to seek a solution; nuisances we accept more readily. Think of some of the nuisances you are incorrectly labelling as problems and replace them into the correct category.
- One of the main aims in life is to live in the present. Often we have a tendency to wander into the future with 'what if?'
  − Would you class yourself as a future worrier? Think of something you are presently worrying about and put it into the category of possibility or probability.
- One of the ways to help improve our confidence is to be comfortable feeling vulnerable. Many people avoid this feeling as they are too sensitive.
  − Do you know the feeling of vulnerability? Could you allow yourself to feel vulnerable and in doing so realise you can survive it and hence have no need to avoid it in future?

20

Building Confidence

When we anticipate a situation outside our 'comfort zone' (see Chapter 21 Facing Our Fears), it is often necessary to build confidence in order to deal with it successfully.

The building process occurs in a stepwise fashion (hence the term building confidence) and often at an unconscious level. The following is a pattern which may be helpful.

1. Being aware that a situation is going to occur causing you fear and insecurity.
2. Focus on what you would like to achieve – the aim, outcome or goal.
3. Write down the steps required to achieve that outcome. The *actual* things you need to do.
4. Ask yourself if your needs are reasonable. You may need to use this fact if negotiations are required.
5. Think of the positive results that will occur when you achieve your goal.
6. Put your task into a suitable perspective. Don't raise the plank (Chapter 23 Walking The Plank).
7. If your task includes dealing with another person, change the words confronting, arguing, winning or losing to 'negotiating'.

8. Be aware of your feelings. If there is fear make a commitment to yourself to 'feel the fear and do it anyway'.
9. Spend time imagining the negotiating process in your mind. Have a successful outcome in your imagination; one where everyone wins. Focus on your flexibility, your ability to express wishes and feelings and also listen to others. Be aware if you are closing your mind to alternative options.
10. Each day go through stage 9 so you are both 'incubating' your ideas and having a dress rehearsal for the future event.

Eleanor was 35 when she came to see me for help with her driving test. She had lost her confidence after failing twice before.

We went through the 10 steps to provide a confidence framework for the next test scheduled in three months time.

1. She was aware of the situation – that was why she was seeing me.
2. Her aim was to pass the driving test.
3. To pass the test she needed to be calmer. In her previous tests she had panicked. She needed to slow her mind down as it raced as soon as she met the examiner. She needed to reduce her fear of failure.
4. She felt her needs were reasonable.
5. When she passed the test she would buy a new car. She had decided on the one she would choose and had saved enough money for this.
6. She was able to put her aim into perspective with the rest of her life. She realised it was not nearly as important as such things as her children's health or the relationship with her husband. She lowered the plank to reduce the pressure of her task.
7. Not relevant.
8. She closed her eyes and focused on all the feelings associated with the test. She imagined proceeding and succeeding even though the experience may have associated fear. She made sure in her imagination that the fear didn't increase to panic.

9. & 10. She spent time each day focusing on the test and remaining calm as she went through the course. She learnt a relaxation exercise and practised reducing tension whenever it occurred.

Some months later Eleanor sent me a note enclosing a photo of her new car. She wrote that everything went according to plan except for a slight hiccup when she stalled and nearly panicked.

She had used the weeks to build her confidence, following the routine we discussed each day and pretending she was doing the test whenever she had a lesson with her driving instructor.

Many people focus on previous 'failures' to reinforce the belief they are no good. These past experiences are viewed through a 'reterospectoscope' – an imaginary machine that helps us to look at the past with the benefit of hindsight.

Looking at past experiences and telling ourselves we should have done better is a sure way to reduce confidence. Each past experience is a rung in the ladder of learning helping us to get where we are. If we undermine our previous behaviour with criticism and blame, we are breaking those rungs and instead of climbing we will slide down.

To build confidence we need to examine in a positive light, the attitude, effort and behaviour we had in the past.

We did the best we could with the choices available to us at the time.

Realising what we learnt from those experiences is much more helpful than criticising ourselves and focusing on so-called 'failures'. Being generous towards our efforts and attempts in the past provides us with strength to deal with the present and face the future.

Having a *role model* is one way of boosting confidence.

The theory is very simple. Choose someone who has the confidence and qualities you need to overcome your fears. Imagine what that person would do in your situation, then pretend to be that person, confidence and courage will follow.

The person you choose can be anyone – a friend, a teacher from the past, a film-star, a cartoon character, even a therapist.

Ask yourself, 'What would that person do, say, react, if they were in the situation I'm concerned about?'

It is a little like playing a character in a play. You immerse yourself in them, get under their skins, know what they think. Doing this with your role model focuses your attention away from the fear. It is a learning process, you gain support and confidence from the character you choose.

Eileen was being picked on by her boss at work. She was nervous every time he came into her part of the office. She changed from a reasonably confident person to a mouse whenever he approached.

The constant fear was having its repercussions – her sleeping pattern was disturbed, she was drinking more and was noticeably more nervous than usual.

We discussed various aspects of her problem and I asked her if she knew anyone who could handle her situation better than she was.

She thought for a moment and then said her friend Joanne certainly could.

We discussed the concept of a role model and she agreed to spend the next week thinking how Joanne would react to her boss' actions.

At the next visit she said she had learnt a lot about her behaviour and believed she was ready to pretend she was Joanne. She knew what Joanne would say and how she would respond if she was picked on.

The following week Eileen came in looking upset.

'Didn't it work?' I asked.

'I didn't get the chance to put it into practice. For some strange reason he didn't pick on me at all last week. It's the first week in months he hasn't had a go at me.'

'Perhaps you were sending different vibrations and he picked them up.'

'Perhaps. I was all ready to fight and nothing happened.'

Over the following weeks Eileen's boss occasionally made upsetting comments but she was able to deflect them or say what she believed Joanne would say.

She stopped seeing me after this, saying she felt comfortable whatever happened. If the boss had stopped picking on her that was great and if he started she was ready for him.

A practical technique to help build confidence is called 'the bridge of opportunity'.

The accompanying diagram explains what is involved. In order for it to work for you, you need to put work into it. Just looking at the diagram and exercise and saying 'that's very interesting, I agree with that' will not cause any improvement. It needs to be incorporated into your daily activities just like brushing your teeth.

Give yourself 10 minutes each day to focus on what you need to get from A to B, what will help this and what has been hindering it. Write things down in your exercise book to reinforce the process, just as you would for work or your diary.

The Bridge of Opportunity

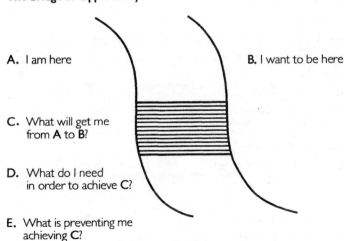

A. I am here

B. I want to be here

C. What will get me from **A** to **B**?

D. What do I need in order to achieve **C**?

E. What is preventing me achieving **C**?

1. Write down what A, B and C mean to you.
2. Write down a list of things represented by D and E.
3. Each day write down what you can do to achieve C and make a commitment to do it.
4. Be aware of what happens during the day that is represented by E and create ways to overcome these.

There are many ways to build confidence. All of them require a knowledge of what to do and the time and effort to put this knowledge into practice.

It's not necessarily going to succeed straight away, but there is a great deal of learning to be acquired during the process of trying. One major thing you will learn is that no matter what happens you *will* survive the ordeal and the fears will have been much greater than the actual event.

Unless we change direction we are likely to end up where we are heading.

ZEN SAYING

CONFIDENCE BOOSTERS

- Building confidence consists of small actions that add to your confidence.
  - Think of a situation that you have avoided in the past but feel you are *almost* able to do – this is the *aim*.
  - Write down what you *actually require* to progress towards *fulfilling* doing what you have avoided in the past.
  - Focus on the *positive outcomes* of your action not on the fears and concerns.
  - Be aware of your feelings and again focus on the positive feelings you will have when you complete your aim.
  - Spend some quiet time imagining the sequence of events that will occur to lead to your aim (a dress rehearsal).

- Make a time frame as to when you are going to do what is required.
- Just *do* it and praise yourself when it is completed whatever the outcome.
- Focus on another aspect of your life you would like to improve.
  - Choose a role model whom you believe would be confident and comfortable with this aspect.
  - During the day imagine how your role model would act, feel and speak.
  - 'Brainwash' yourself with your role model's attitude so you can feel as they would.
  - Put your 'brainwashing' into practice.
- Reread the 'Bridge of Opportunity'.
  - Write down what A, B and C mean to you.
  - Write a list of things represented by D & E.
  - Each day focus on what you need to achieve C. Start with small aims and build up as your confidence grows.

21

Facing Our Fears

Life can be seen as series of challenges beginning the day we were delivered from the safety and security of the womb; facing a completely different world of light, sound and touch is indeed a challenge.

Initially our only survival tool is crying – to attract others to our plight. As we grow we develop other means of gaining control and so the process of building confidence begins.

The parental role is two-fold – to help us and also to direct us to help ourselves. Initially parents must do everything and gradually we are given responsibility and we are allowed to learn (mostly from mistakes). Each time we learn something we add a grain of sand to the scales of confidence. Our whole system recognises we can do things, are capable and less dependent.

Little by little, this process continues – challenge, attempt to overcome it, failure, repeated attempts, success and (hopefully) praise followed by self-praise. Each step along the journey increases our confidence, and situations that were difficult become easier.

The mind takes on board these experiences and new neural circuits are laid down in the brain – like updating a computer. People that have the most difficulty in life are those that don't learn from their experiences. The basis of this behaviour is a maintenance of a theory in spite of the evidence. One of the most important mechanisms is one of survival. It is as if on a very deep level alarm systems are set up to provide security. These may develop due to circumstances in childhood where situations cause extreme fear.

A child believing it will be abandoned; continuous caution from a parent; a terrifying experience, all will set up the survival mechanism in the unconscious.

This mechanism is generally of the form 'don't do something as it is dangerous and life-threatening.' As the person grows and the situation may be safe, the underlying protective mechanism prevents learning in order to maintain the theory of danger.

The saying 'better the devil you know than the one you don't' explains why people are loathe to try anything new and if they do then they regard it as a 'one off' and avoid learning from it.

The force of fear causes people to hold on to outdated information. They know they are still alive so why risk trying anything new. The fact that they have limitations and difficulties is not strong enough to take the risk of new attitudes.

The process of learning about our abilities, gaining strength from that knowledge and being more adaptable when a similar situation is encountered is the process of gaining confidence. In fact what we are doing each time we accept a challenge is *overcoming fear*. It is important that the size of the fear is suitable to allow us to face it.

When I meet adults whose basic problem is lack of confidence, I ask them if they ever learnt to ride a bike, swim, ride a horse, roller-skate, drive a car. Often they say, 'No, we were too frightened' or 'Our parents wouldn't allow it'.

These adults have used the 'techniques of avoidance' to get through life. Many parents support this approach through fear of what may happen to their children. They want the best for their children, protect them from harm and in the process protect them from many situations that would enable growth of confidence.

The constant refrain from such parents is 'Don't . . .'

- 'Don't get your feet wet, you will catch cold.'
- 'Don't go near that puppy, it will bite you.'
- 'Don't try roller-skating, you'll break your ankle.'
- 'Don't go in the water, you'll drown.'

All these admonitions may be well meaning but the underlying message is 'The world is a dangerous place, terrible things will happen to you if you take risks.'

The receiver of such messages learns to approach every new situation with fear as his overriding emotion. He is on guard, prepared for danger, in a defensive mood and labelling every challenge as a danger to his survival.

Every stranger is a potential murderer, every car an accident, every new situation a calamity waiting to happen. As children grow with these messages their circle of activity remains small and protected. Their first action is to avoid, retreat, defend, say 'no' and the potential to explore, experiment and learn is nullified.

The message 'everything new is dangerous' stays for years. On an unconscious level the brainwashing by over-protective parents goes deep into the back of the mind. Adults trained in this way automatically say 'no' when offered a new choice. These unfortunate people find great difficulty in overcoming their brainwashing in spite of positive experiences that contradict it.

Charles was 50 and has been in the same job for 20 years. He has been offered promotion many times but became anxious, depressed and panicked and was unable to accept it. His firm no longer suggested promotion and he had come to terms with the fact that he would remain where he was until he retired.

In fact he hadn't completely come to terms with his inability to accept promotion. That was why he came to see me. Part of him wanted the benefits of a superior job but his fears battled with this part and won the battle each time.

There were many other aspects to his life where this fear prevented him doing things. He lived alone, had never formed a long-term relationship, his hobbies were solitary and he often felt anxious and shy.

He described his childhood as 'living in cotton-wool'. He was the only child of over-protective parents, always cautioned about calamities which might have befallen him.

The normal challenges of childhood were kept from him. He wasn't allowed to stay with friends, never rode a bike, was driven to and from school, didn't have a pet and his mother stayed at the parties he went to, to ensure he had a good time.

His mother's over-protectiveness stemmed from the fact that she had lost a brother in a car accident when he was 10 years old. Her parents never overcame their grief and the message constantly repeated within the family was 'If only we'd been more protective, this would never have happened.'

Charles' mother carried this motto into her marriage, and spent much energy ensuring the same fate wouldn't befall her. She kept Charles in cotton-wool preventing him exploring, making mistakes or taking risks as this was dangerous living.

This environment did not help Charles adapt to real life when he left home. He was shy, tentative, had difficulty with relationships (mum had warned him about girls) and could not bring himself to be assertive.

As he grew, saw others having more fun, being more successful, having more experiences, he realised his tuition was unsuitable but couldn't shake off the warnings stored deep in his mind.

He tried hard to be forceful and independent, but his emotions made that impossible. He panicked, his hands sweated, his heart raced and his voice trembled when he tried to be assertive. So he gave up.

My job with Charles was to support him in the process of risk-taking. He and I worked out a plan. He was to write out the smallest risks he wished to achieve and I was to help support him in doing so. No matter how strange or small his risks were, we treated them with complete respect.

In the first week he agreed to ask someone in the street for a light (Charles was a smoker). His mother had said he risked being mugged by taking such a frightening action. He did it and was pleased with the friendly response. So pleased that he asked five people for a light in the first week. He was delighted to report his success and we discussed his next task, which was to ask a woman in his local pub what the time was.

Charles had a favourite seat in the corner of the pub. He always drank alone and was occasionally joined by other locals, but he admitted to me he felt uncomfortable by these 'intruders'.

He felt this new task would be almost impossible. His fantasy was that the woman would scream rape if he asked the time. After a long discussion with me he said he would need an extra pint but would have a go.

His next visit revealed he had again succeeded; no police arrived when he asked the woman for the time. In fact, she chatted to him for a minute or so before he scurried back to his corner.

Week after week, Charles continued his tasks. Generally he was able to diminish the warnings from the past and instil his present-day experiences. He came out of his cotton-wool. He did not become a lion but was closer to a Labrador than a mouse . . .

What can we learn from Charles' story?

1. The learning he received in childhood was 'the world is a dangerous place, don't take risks, terrible things will happen to you if you stray from the tightrope of your present situation'.
2. This message had kept him immobilised in the same job for 20 years in spite of encouragement to improve his situation.
3. In order to help Charles out of his circle of comfort it was important to select tasks that were suitable for his state of confidence. He and I worked out risks which had previously been just beyond his ability.
4. By performing these (simple) tasks Charles learnt a great deal. They were like the first steps a toddler takes. They

change the world even though they are minimal procedures.

5. The hope with Charles was that as he completed one task after another he would enter the world of reality and leave behind the artificial world created by his over-protective mother.

6. Each step Charles took would be helpful. Even if he didn't succeed, he learnt that he could survive and the horrific things described by his mother just didn't occur.

7. The pace of progress depended solely on his ability to cope with each task; as they became more difficult he became more reluctant to take risks so the process slowed accordingly.

8. The level that Charles reached was again related to the balance between his desires and the difficulty in achieving these. If I had pushed him too fast or too far he would have regressed and found the therapy too intimidating. I had to let Charles be the driver; I was the guide and supporter.

9. In fact he improved to a level where he joined a small group of friends at the pub. He joined in the quiz night and darts games and at this level he decided to leave therapy. He had accepted his job status and was focusing on the benefits – pension, not too demanding, knows everyone at that level.

10. The main achievement for Charles was peace of mind. He made progress in many areas but the main benefit from therapy was accepting himself as he was. He learnt a lot about himself in the process and also learnt the world was not the terrifying place his mother had described.

Facing your fears is a basic rule for emotional growth. Mistakes/failures are really the stepping stones to success. Falling off a bike and grazing an arm is not a problem. The graze will heal in a few days, the learning remains for life.

A wise doctor in America had four children and from an early age they slept in different beds every week. Sometimes they slept on the floor, other times in a tent or a couch. Some nights they slept with their heads facing one way, other nights the opposite way.

He told me he arranged this for a special reason. They would have to cope with a wide variety of change in their lives and the message he was giving them was that change was normal and they needn't be fazed by it.

Changing the label from 'problem' to 'challenge' helps us mobilise our resources in a completely different way. If learning to ride a bike is a problem undermined by the parental advice 'Don't fall off and break you leg', we will be frightened, not only of falling off but the recrimination that will follow in the form of 'I told you so!'

Approaching the same situation as a challenge supported by 'Let's see if you can ride ten yards before falling off' is a completely different situation. Receiving praise and support if you do fall off is a far cry from 'I told you so' and encourages you to try again.

Developing a 'have-a-go' attitude is a great partner in life. Developing a motto 'Better to have tried and failed than not to have tried at all' ensures the 'have-a-go' attitude, the 'Why not?' as opposed to the 'Why?' question.

If we regard our ability to cope with things, our circle of comfort, as a circle thus:

facing fears and challenges, taking risks, learning from mistakes enlarges the circle:

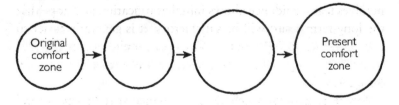

Facing fears, why not, have a go.

The circumference of the circle is the cutting edge, the risk-taking area. Inside the circle are things we can do, feel comfortable with; those outside the circle are things beyond us, too frightening, too risky.

By facing fears, having a go, we enlarge our world, develop more choices, our pathway is wider and easier and our confidence grows.

On the other hand, if we use the *technique of avoidance* our world shrinks:

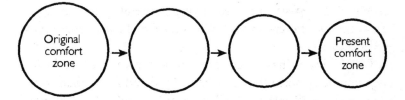

Avoidance, playing safe, why? Better the devil you know than the one you don't, don't try in case you fail.

With this attitude we lose choices, our world closes in around us, our comfort zone decreases, things become more difficult, our energy and enthusiasm decreases.

Techniques of avoidance develop in a number of ways. Many times I hear people say 'anything for a peaceful life'. These people have the least peaceful life of all. They believe 'it will sort itself out' even though over the years this is obviously not the case.

It is often 'easier' to avoid than do something. Taking a risk involves fear, avoidance allows initial gratification and hope that the long-term result will be satisfactory. It is generally easier to ask 'Why?' than 'Why not?' 'Why not?' implies a commitment to do something. 'Why?' defers action and places the onus on the questioner.

People remember when their avoidance was beneficial and forget the times when it resulted in failure. They rely on hope and others to ensure success rather than taking responsibility themselves.

Life is often a struggle out of our comfort zone as it was when we were expelled from the womb, as it is for a chicken when pecking its way out of an egg, as it is every morning when the alarm rings and we'd rather stay in bed.

It's easy to see why people stay in their comfort zone – it's comfortable! The aim is to have a balance where challenges are balanced with the comfort of the status quo.

Somewhere along the way our confidence is intertwined between the seeking and the accepting.

The lust for comfort, that stealthy thing that enters the house as a guest, and then becomes a host, and then a master.

KAHEIL GIBRAN

CONFIDENCE BOOSTERS

- People who use avoidance techniques tell themselves 'I'll start tomorrow; anything for a peaceful life; what will people think if I do that?; what if I make a mistake?; they may be angry if I say that; it will sort itself out.'

  How often do you use avoidance as a technique to deal with difficulties?

  How successful is it?

- The phrase 'facing your fears' is often used when advice is given. In practice it means feeling frightened about doing or saying something and doing it anyway. The process has three stages:
  - Recognising you need to do or say something.
  - Realise you feel frightened to do so, and have an urge to avoid it.
  - Doing it anyway even though you feel fear.

Choose something that fits into category (1).

Be aware of the fear (2). And do it anyway (3) even though your feelings are directing you towards avoidance.

• Some people respond with a 'Why?' when asked to do something. Others say 'Why not?' and do it.

Are you a 'Why' or a 'Why not' person?

22

Being Aware

In psychological terms our minds are run by our unconscious when we are born (unaware) and our progress through life is one of becoming more conscious (aware).

Conscious behaviour means we are in control, are following our wishes and can accept responsibility for them. Unconscious behaviour is beyond our control, is related to our inner world (see Chapter 26 Our Inner Worlds) and often is not in line with our aims.

A comparison may be made with a man who behaves respectfully when sober but changes into an abusive person when drunk. The next day he may not recall his behaviour and accepts no responsibility for it.

It is as if the unconscious has taken over once conscious control is removed by the alcohol. By becoming aware of the effect alcohol has on his behaviour he is at the start of the journey to resolve it.

Being aware is a two-fold obligation – to be aware of ourselves and also of others.

Many people tell me they are very good at solving other people's problems but no good at dealing with their own. This is because they are able to view others from a suitable perspective

IF YOU IMAGINE FLOATING UP AND LOOKING AT YOURSELF
DOING THINGS THEN YOU ARE STARTING TO BECOME AWARE

but are so entwined with their own difficulties they can't see the wood for the trees.

Being aware is similar to the term used by Eastern gurus – enlightenment. One way of regarding it is viewing yourself from another place. If you imagine floating up and looking at yourself doing things then you are starting to become aware.

This is a very helpful process and disentangles us from all our hang ups, gives us confidence and reduces fear. It is an old concept as illustrated by many sayings in our language:

- 'Take a good look at yourself.'
- 'You should always be able to laugh at yourself.'
- 'He's so involved in his own thoughts and feelings that he is missing the point.'
- 'If only we could get him out of himself, his life would be so much easier.'
- 'He is his own worst enemy.'

Tim found it difficult to do things. His mind raced in so many directions he was bombarded with choices and could never decide which would be the best one.

He was forever weighing the pros and cons and worried about making a mistake. His friends used to dread asking him to join them as they never knew (neither did he) what he was going to do.

I talked to him about being aware. He found the concept good in theory but had no idea how to put it into practice. I asked him to imagine himself above looking down on himself. The one above was to be the observer – no views, opinions or emotions – to view the Tim below trying to make up his mind.

At the time of the consultation he was worried about the decision to ask a girl to a party next weekend or not. I asked him to sit quietly with his eyes closed and observe himself having difficulties making that decision

'It's ridiculous,' he exclaimed after a few minutes, 'Why all that fuss over such a simple decision?'

I laughed and said, 'It looks like the scales are dropping from your eyes.'

He laughed too and promised to practise drifting up to view himself every day.

I would like to say Tim changed instantly but he didn't. He drifted back into his old habits again and again and I kept helping him hoist himself upwards for a better view.

After many weeks, he said he thought he had the hang of it and was going to continue practising his 'self-elevation' as he called it, on his own.

Being aware of others means not allowing your perspective to be tainted by your own views and opinions.

A bird-watcher spends hours observing birds. He doesn't say one is a good bird and the other a bad one. He just observes and records their behaviour and accepts it as typical of that species. His involvement is in the observing, not judging. He accepts the bird as it is and enjoys what he sees from a neutral point of view.

That is awareness of others: observing them from a neutral point of view without judgement or values – they are what they are. You don't need to give them advice as you are accepting they are doing the best they can to be themselves. I personally find this very difficult to do. I have a deep-seated belief I know what is best for others. As I get older I realise this is far from the truth but the tape keeps playing in my head. I suppose if I was a bird-watcher I'd rush out and tell the bird there was a big worm over by the tree.

There is a phenomenon which occurs when observers are involved. I have encountered it on a number of occasions when I have run workshops on psychotherapy.

I have asked for a volunteer to sit in the front on a chair next to me so I can demonstrate some technique. The volunteer talks about himself and I challenge some of his beliefs. Often he may cry if sensitive areas are brought to the surface.

On a number of occasions, someone in the group has become very angry with me saying I had hurt and upset the volunteer and I was insensitive to their feelings. I have been concerned by this criticism and apologised to the volunteer. Every time the volunteer has said he felt really good and found the experience very helpful and uplifting.

The observer in the group was not receiving the same experience as the volunteer. He may well have been saying to himself, 'If that was me, I'd feel hurt and upset.' He was viewing the situation from a biased point of view and thus received distorted information.

Many people have 'mental filters' that change their appreciation of a situation. Because of their early experience they need to filter out certain aspects of behaviour as they are too painful. They often use the 'dark glasses of negativity' to shield themselves from hurt and in doing so distort the experience.

Alan's parents argued constantly when he was growing up. The sound of raised voices caused him to become anxious and upset and he made sure he avoided the possibility of this occurring.

This mental filter caused him much concern whenever healthy disagreements occurred at work or at home with his new wife.

His filter told him 'arguing is wrong and results in tears and divorce', and he was unable to see that it is a normal way people resolve difficulties. We redefined the word as 'discussions and negotiations' and he felt better about accepting behaviour labelled that way.

Over some months of therapy Alan was able to reduce his filter and still feel safe. We had role-play sessions where we 'negotiated and discussed' in a heated way subjects he felt strongly about. He realised it did not destroy our relationship and result in hurt and guilt.

He began practising a little at work to express views that differed from others. He was surprised that his world didn't crumble the way he had observed with his parents.

He became more *aware* how his mental filter had biased and restricted his views and was able to realise he could still feel safe while disagreeing.

Our attitudes and perspectives dictate how we feel. Often two opposing attitudes may be both correct yet lead us in completely opposite directions.

Looking at the National Lottery, one point of view may be 'Someone has got to win it, so I'm going to buy a ticket.' Another view could be 'The chance of winning is like being struck by lightning twice on the same day, I'm not going to buy a ticket.' Both these views are correct, yet they have a completely opposite outcome on the people thinking them.

Being open to other views and attitudes helps us become aware of different possibilities. It doesn't mean that the views *we* held were wrong but that we are able to make more choices by being open to alternatives.

The concept of being aware – observing yourself from above – helps so much with confidence. When we are caught up, as Tim was, in going here and there in our minds, our confidence is eroded in the process.

If we imagine a rat in a maze trying to find its way to some cheese, we could see him scurrying hither and thither, becoming more and more confused and less and less confident as time went on. If he could imagine rising up and seeing the maze as it was, his course would be easy.

We carry with us tapes from the past – from our parents, teachers, etc. – and as these conflicting tapes continue to play we become caught in a dilemma, our decision-making abilities confused, and our confidence suffers.

By cutting through all the 'red tape' and viewing ourselves from above the direction becomes much clearer because it is not cluttered by past emotions and doctrines. The viewer part of yourself is uninhibited by the direction of others. If you were stuck in a traffic jam never knowing when you'll get home and someone took you out of your car and lifted you up in a helicopter, it would become easy to assess the outcome of the traffic jam. You would see what had caused it (perhaps an accident), how many roads were blocked, the tow trucks at the scene, etc. It wouldn't necessarily make the time home any shorter but you would not be troubled by the confusing and irritating questions you were asking yourself before.

Meditation

One specific form of awareness comes from the practice of meditation. On a number of occasions in this book I have suggested exercises involving quiet time, inner focus or meditation.

The basis of meditation is to still the active mind (the 'monkey mind' that continually flits from one subject to another) so that peace and tranquillity can envelope the mind from a lower level. This calmness has many benefits including insight into oneself or the subject you are meditating on.

The process to achieve a meditative state varies depending on which form of meditation you choose but the principles are very similar.

1. Allow yourself time when you will not be interrupted. Ensure your partner or children are aware that you are having this quiet time and will not disturb you. Make sure the phone is off the hook or the answer machine is on with the ringing tone turned off.

2. Choose a place that is pleasant and suitable for your quiet time. Some people meditate during their lunch time in their cars, others meditate before work or on returning from work.

3. In order to get into the habit of meditating use the same time each day. It is preferable not to use the time in bed before you go to sleep as you are likely to be tired and drift off to sleep.

4. There are many positions people choose – the most popular is sitting in a comfortable chair with your head supported, or lying on the floor.

5. Breathing is an important component of most forms of meditation. As breathing is natural and rhythmic it creates a good basis for focusing your attention. Allow the breathing to occur naturally and focus on the exhalation to allow yourself to float down.

6. Have your eyes closed so that you are focusing internally.

7. Move from a trying, doing, analysing state to a being, accepting state. Allow your thoughts to flit from one subject to another without trying to direct them, in time this process will slow down and you will begin to move into the meditative state – a calm, peaceful and relaxed state.

8. If you are using this quiet time to explore some aspect of your mind have the subject in your mind as you begin the process as if you are asking some part of your mind to be aware of this from a deeper perspective. You don't need to continually focus on this subject as you will have sown the seed already. For example, if you wished to review the previous day in this relaxed state then this intention would be stated to yourself as you started the meditation process.

9. Remain in the quiet state for about 20 minutes. Your internal clock is very accurate and will let you know when the time has passed. Some days you will find you remain for a shorter time, other days a longer time.
10. When you are ready to come out of the meditative state, gradually drift upwards until you feel your eyes open. Sit quietly for a few minutes to adjust to the transition into the conscious active state.

Doing this exercise on a regular basis is very helpful in a number of different ways. It gives you the necessary quiet time to balance the activities of the rest of the day. It allows you to take a different perspective on external situations and even your own personality. It provides time for the creative part of your mind to supply you with new ideas to discover about yourself.

I'm at home and at ease on a track that I know not,
and restless and lost on a road that I know.

HENRY LAWSON
AUSTRALIAN POET

CONFIDENCE BOOSTERS

- Using the directions from the chapter make time for yourself to do a half-hour meditation. At first learn the process without any definite aim, appreciating the change from the *trying* state to the *being* state.

- When you have spent a number of sessions learning to meditate, choose a subject you would like to view from a different perspective and use that as a focus for your quiet time.

- Choose a person you have difficulties with. Be aware of your feelings towards them. Now observe them as a bird-watcher would observe a bird – no shoulds, comparisons or judgements. Use your observation to see them in a factual way rather than an emotional one.

23

Walking the Plank

There are not many things that matter in life, *really* matter. Too often we are concerned about events that a few days later will be completely forgotten.

Adrian was distraught and depressed due to a prolonged legal battle with his neighbours. This battle had grumbled on for four years. He did not speak to his neighbour, had already paid thousands of pounds in legal fees and the conflict was still unresolved.

What was in dispute was the fence-line. His neighbour claimed it was two inches away from where it should be – two inches!

The courts are full of angry neighbours screaming about things of similar magnitude (or minitude). In the grand scale of things is two inches on a fence-line important? What would the neighbour do with the extra two inches of land?

There is a saying: 'Many are stubborn in pursuit of the pathway, few in pursuit of the goal!'

We get lost in the battle and forget the outcome. We raise the stakes of differences to such a height we are prepared to spend thousands and waste four years for two inches.

In order to overcome challenges we often need to put them in perspective. The majority of fights are about things that are not really important. If we put the hurdle too high it will be difficult to jump it, bringing it back to a suitable height means the task is so much easier.

Sophie came to see me and burst into tears in the first 10 minutes. Life was just *too* difficult, she couldn't cope, she didn't know the answers, she was exhausted and tense. She kept repeating the phrase 'I'm frightened of not getting it right and the children will go off the rails.'

Her driving emotion was *fear of making a mistake*. The main problem for Sophie was her two children, Tom and Chris, aged 12 and 14. She was continually screaming at them and they wouldn't do anything she asked.

When we got down to the facts it became apparent that Sophie placed too much importance on every aspect of the household.

Tom was supposed to do piano practise each night and he didn't. Chris watched too much television and didn't get to bed till 9.30 pm. Neither of them cleaned their shoes and their rooms were a mess. Their table manners were terrible and they constantly fought with each other.

Sophie had made things *really* matter when in the grand scale of things they didn't. We discussed each of the boys activities (or inactivities) which caused her to see red. I asked her how important would they be in 10 years' time. I asked her to focus on the *good* things about Tom and Chris, to minimise their irritations and put things into perspective.

I talked to her about the plank technique. I asked her to imagine a plank four foot wide on the floor. I asked her to stand up and imagine walking along the plank focusing on two feelings:

1. Could she do it?
2. How did she feel?

She proceeded to walk on the imaginary plank on the carpet then sat down.

'Can you do it?' I asked.

'Yes.'

'How did it feel?'

'OK. No problem.'

'So, we know you can walk on a four foot wide plank. I could give you a certificate for this. Now imagine we put the plank between two sky-scrapers and I asked you (as we both know you can do it) to walk on the plank between the sky-scrapers.'

'I wouldn't do it. I'd be too frightened. I'd be terrified I'd fall.'

'But we both know you are capable, you've shown it here.'

'Yes, but I couldn't do it up there.'

'That's right. Neither could anyone else. And that is what you are doing at home. You are raising the plank too high and therefore can't cope with it. I'd suggest you bring the plank down to floor level. All the things you say about Tom and Chris are perfectly normal and healthy for boys of that age. Allowing them to be themselves more, giving them more responsibility, not worrying too much about these things will make life easier for everyone – especially you.'

There is a Zen saying 'If you want to control your sheep and goats put them in the largest paddock you possess.'

Sophie wasn't very happy about our discussion but agreed to give it a try. She would tell Tom that she was not going to supervise his piano practise and if the teacher wasn't satisfied lessons would stop. She would close the door to their bedroom so as not to know what disaster lay inside. If Chris was tired from staying up late that would be his problem; he had to get up for school on time and Sophie would be checking with the teacher that his work was satisfactory.

After a number of hiccups, Sophie became more relaxed about her boys. She backed off, and focused on their strengths rather than their faults. In some strange way, the boys responded in a positive manner and a form of peace settled on the household.

That's not to say that everything was smooth. Many times Sophie had to force herself to 'lower the plank', go into another room, count to 10 and from time to time even have an extra glass of wine.

Life is a lot easier when we get things into a suitable perspective. We are cocooned in our way of life and believe we are suffering if all is not going according to plan. By achieving a wider perspective we are able to see that our catastrophes are not nearly so bad. Our confidence is often dependent on the perspective we choose.

A wonderful book, helpful in putting things into perspective is called *The Diving-Bell and the Butterfly*. It was written by a remarkable Frenchman Jean-Dominique Bauby (see Further Reading), who had a stroke, after which the only muscle he could move was his left eye-lid.

He dictated his book using his left eye-lid only! What an amazing feat in itself, but even more remarkable is the warmth and optimism in his life story as he tells it.

When you are ranting and raving about the difficulties you are encountering, I suggest you read Jean-Dominique Bauby's book – it has a great way of helping put things into perspective.

Some people have great difficulties with decisions. They go backwards and forwards between the choices, becoming frustrated, weary and losing confidence in the process.

What often happens is that they are raising the plank too high, placing too great a value on the decision they are attempting to resolve. By lowering the plank the choice becomes so much easier.

We follow messages in our mind, messages that have been taught to us. People that focus on trivial tasks, giving them great importance have often received the message when they were growing up – 'you must get it right'.

This message does not discriminate between what is important and what is not. The 'getting it right' is a measure of their self-worth – praised for getting it right and criticised for mistakes.

The trivial aspects of life therefore take on a much greater significance and the plank is raised out of all proportion.

Small misdemeanours or mistakes by their children become items of major importance. Life is serious and normal mishaps become catastrophes.

Albert came to see me worried about his 16-year-old son, Jonathan.

'Dr Roet, I'm very concerned about Jonathan. He is at boarding-school and his teacher has contacted me to inform me Jonathan is in trouble for stealing. I would like you to see him and see if you can help prevent him going off the rails.'

'Has he stolen many times before?'

'No, this is the first time but you can never be sure where it may lead.'

'What did he steal?'

'A Coca-Cola and a cake from the tuck-shop!'

'A Coca-Cola and a cake!! Do you think it is necessary for him to see someone like me because of a Coca-Cola and a cake?'

'Well, it's stealing, isn't it?'

'Yes, I agree it's stealing and he shouldn't have done that, but if you bring him to see me you may be making a much bigger deal of it than it really is. It may have been a school-boy prank that he did with his mates. Do you think you could spend some time talking and listening to him without making it a major crime and learn what went on that led him to take the cake and drink?'

Albert had put Jonathan's misdemeanour into a major category of crime and so had caused himself great worry and concern. He rang me some days later thanking me for helping him get the experience into perspective and relating the fact that he and Jonathan had had a 'man to man' discussion which was really beneficial for both.

Most decisions we make in life are not *that* important that we need to make ourselves sick in the process of trying to decide. By reducing the value and importance of our choices we waste less energy in making sure we make the right decision.

In my experience life plays tricks anyway and, after all the trouble we go to in making decisions, something occurs which changes the picture completely.

A wise Polish farmer was working away in the fields when a wild horse galloped through his gate and into the paddock. He closed the gate and continued with his work.

Neighbours came in and exclaimed 'How lucky you are, a beautiful horse for nothing.'

The farmer said, 'May be so may be not, I really don't know.'

A week later the farmer's son aged 18 went riding on the horse, fell off and broke his arm. The neighbours came to console him.

'What bad luck you are having. Your son with a broken arm all because of that horse.'

'May be so may be not, I really don't know,' came the quiet reply.

Two weeks later the Polish army came around to conscript soldiers for the war. All the young men in town had to go off and fight except the farmer's son who was excluded with his broken arm.

The neighbours wailed and moaned and came to the farmer, 'What a lucky man you are, etc.'

This story places a different perspective on outcomes. By lowering the values we can see nature at work, put less pressure on ourselves to make decisions and get on with the job of enjoying life. Whatever crisis confronts us today, some day it will be just a memory.

Today's newspaper crisis is tomorrow's fish and chip wrapping.

CONFIDENCE BOOSTERS

- Walking the plank is a concept to enable you to get things into perspective. Too often we magnify problems so that they are difficult to deal with. Actually go through the exercise of walking on an imaginary plank on the floor. Note how it feels. Then sit down and realise how much more frightening it would feel if the plank was between two sky-scrapers.

- Think of some situations where you get a similar feeling to the plank between the sky-scrapers. Now alter the perspective so that the plank is lowered. How important will that situation be in five years' time? What is the worst outcome and how likely is that?

24

Accepting Your Process Curve

People and animals are creatures of habit. We react to situations in a similar manner each time we experience them. We have our own *pattern* of response even though the individual situations may differ in content. Our reaction is part of our nature and I call this reaction a 'process curve'.

The process curve is a graph plotting the process we go through to deal with what happens to us. It is a habitual pattern we have used successfully (or unsuccessfully) in the past and we are a slave to it rather than vice versa.

For some, their process curve feels like a slide. They are hurtling downwards out of control and fearful of where they will end. Their mind plays tricks with them and thoughts of doom and gloom loom large in front of them. They know it is frightening and they desperately need safety.

Being on a slide for the first time is vastly different from any future occasion. After the first time the process is experienced *consciously* you know the outcome. You've been there before and survived. The next time the fear is greatly diminished because of this knowledge.

Remembering the way previous experiences affected you gives the stability and reassurance you need. 'I've been here before and it got better' allows a safety factor to creep in. This means that the rest of the journey can be carried out with more confidence, optimism and reality.

A classical process curve is the one following personal loss. This may occur because of a broken relationship or death. The steps follow a general pattern involving a number of points on the curve. Some people get stuck at one point and do not allow the healing curve to proceed.

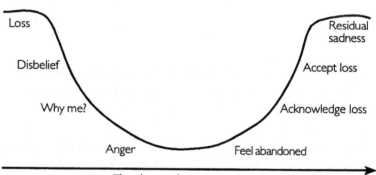

To illustrate the benefit of using the process curve concept, I'll tell you about Tony, a successful businessman. He is a worrier (see Chapter 19 Self-Help Techniques) who sees me when he is 'in a state' about a business transaction. He is drowned in doom and gloom, despondency, failure and guilt.

Over a period of weeks the business venture is resolved successfully, Tony is over his crisis and, as peace and tranquillity returns to his world, I don't see him until the next crisis.

This sequence of events has happened on a regular basis every two to three months for the last few years, nearly always with a successful outcome to his business deal.

I asked Tony to analyse a number of the past situations and plot them on a 'process curve'. This is what Tony produced:

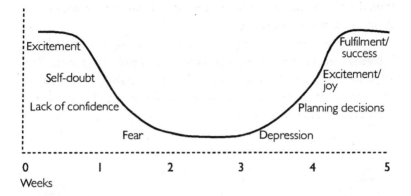

For Tony the curve is repeated in an almost identical manner whenever a major challenge occurs at work. The time factor is also similar on each occasion.

The psychoanalyst Carl Jung said that instead of trying to change our complexes we need to learn to live within them.

Tony and I discussed how he could *accept* his feelings as part of the process, and that this process was part of him like his fingerprint. He didn't need to change it in fact it may be unchangeable. Since the outcome was usually successful he needed to 'go with the flow' and regard each part of his crisis as a fluid point on the curve that led to success.

I asked Tony to recognise that each stage on his graph was not a static state but part of his process of achieving a success-ful outcome. Accepting the total curve, and realising that some of the stages were unpleasant (but not problems), helped Tony realise his various 'downers' were a nuisance to be accepted not a problem to be fixed.

He stuck the graph on his shaving mirror at home and saw the 'whole picture' each morning. He noted where he was on the curve and anticipated the weeks ahead before reaching the 'fulfilment/success' stage.

Tony's process curve had a successful outcome. He realised

that accepting the curve as his fingerprint would allow him to end up where he wanted to be.

Esther's process curve was different. She ended up where she didn't want to be. She was a 40-year-old school-teacher who had immense problems with relationships. She had been married twice to men who turned out be completely unsuitable. Each marriage lasted about two years and consisted of a series of arguments, accusations and physical violence.

She recognised that she played a major role in her relationship problems and one aspect was the way she chose her partner. Apart from her marriages she had been in four long-term relationships, all very similar to her marriages. She was attracted to men who were unsuitable for her temperament, attitude and way of life. I asked Esther to draw her process curve from the time before a relationship till it ended, noting the components which played a role in the shape of the curve. She drew:

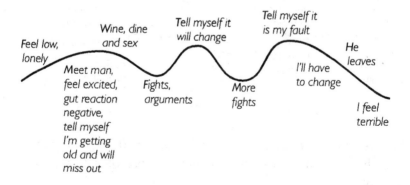

Esther's curve did *not* lead to a successful outcome, in fact she felt *worse* after each encounter. We studied the curve together. She said she felt it was similar with each relationship including the marriages. I asked her to look at the points on the curve that were maintaining the system, points that needed changing to achieve a more positive outcome.

After thinking about my question during the week between visits, she came back with four points she would like to change:

1. Take more notice of her gut reaction on all the initial dates with the man she met.
2. Stop repeating the self-talk that 'he will have to change or I will have to change'. Accept that neither is likely.
3. Stop telling myself I'm old and may miss out. Do the best to enjoy life as it is.
4. Stop telling myself I'm a hopeless person. If I feel this then put some time and effort in to do things that will improve my self-respect.

Esther decided to draw a new curve to stick to her make-up mirror. I asked her to send me a copy and this is what it looked like.

I will accept myself as I am	If I meet a man I will be honest with him	I'll ensure I don't become a victim	I will respect myself throughout
Focus on good things in my life	Trust gut reaction	I'll accept it if it is not working and I will leave	I will learn from the relationship

We are often anxious about what lies ahead. If someone can describe the road ahead we feel much more secure and in control.

A wise doctor treating someone at a roadside accident was of great help when he calmed the anxious victim by saying 'It is going to get worse before it gets better and you *will* be all right in the end.'

Those reassuring words acted as a support to the patient over the next few weeks when he needed to deal with the ups and downs that resulted from the accident.

Liz had a problem with her weight. She had been on diets for years. She would eat according to a strict plan, lose weight, feel better, start to alter her eating and gain weight again.

I discussed with her the innate difficulty in losing weight. There are so many factors involved that it is not a simple process. The mind plays as great a role as the mouth.

I asked her to focus on her process curve relating to her weight and spend the next week plotting the relevant points.

Here is what she drew:

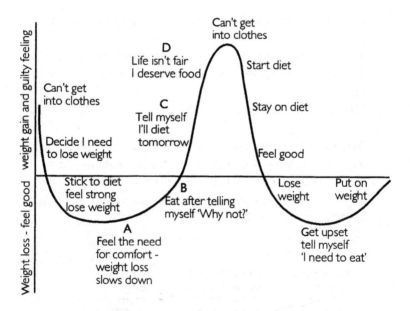

The points she felt were crucial to the direction of her curve were A, B, C and D.

A. Feel the need for comfort and eat
B. Telling myself 'Why not?'
C. Fool myself with 'I'll diet tomorrow.'
D. Tell myself life isn't fair and I deserve food.

We discussed dieting and weight loss and the relevance of the above four points. She agreed she couldn't have her cake and eat it. If she wanted to lose weight she would need to accept the discomfort that entailed. She needed to decide how important it was for her to fit into her clothes.

She thought about this question for a week and returned with a determined attitude to focus on her aim of weight loss and not to continue the see-saw curve which she had followed for some years.

We discussed at length what she could replace A, B, C and D with that would fit in with her aim. She decided on:

A. If I feel the need for comfort I will buy myself a small present.
B. To look at two photos of myself, one fat and one thin.
C. To buy only food that will fit in with the eating pattern I have planned.
D. Life isn't fair and I want to be thin.

Over the following months Liz followed her new curve and found it very helpful. Her eating pattern and weight did fluctuate but only a fraction of what had occurred previously.

When I last saw her I asked her to draw the helpful curve she was following and she drew:

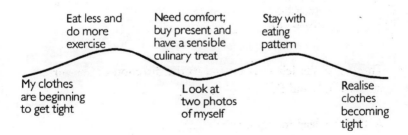

The process curve can be helpful in two separate ways:

1. If from past experience your habit patterns have had successful outcomes in spite of troughs along the way, accept them

and appreciate that they are part of a journey that will end in fulfilment.

2. If your pattern leads to an undesirable outcome look at the stages and find improved alternatives so that the curve has a positive outcome.

Life shapes itself, callous of our control
But proves itself to have been wise at the end.
VITA SACKVILLE-WEST

CONFIDENCE BOOSTERS

- The concept of a process curve implies that situations we experience are part of a continuum rather than static. By learning about the way similar experiences were resolved in the past we can deduce the likely outcome of our present situation.

  Choose a situation that is concerning you and recall similar situations and their outcomes. Are you worrying as if the present situation will not flow in a process curve as previously? Are there some points on the curve that you could change to improve the outcome?

- Many things in our lives repeat themselves – work experiences, relationships, response to our children's behaviour, etc.

  Choose one of these repetitive situations and plot the factors on a curve (see the process curve of Liz). If the outcomes have been successful accept where you are on the curve. If unsuccessful, look at points to improve the outcome.

25

Creative Visualisation

Creative visualisation really means using the imagination in a creative way to deal with difficulties. Many people form pictures in their minds to recall past events or imagine how things will be in the future. This ability is very helpful in many ways.

These pictures create a feeling (see Chapter 26 Our Inner Worlds) and the technique of creative visualisation is to be aware and make use of this link between internal pictures and emotions.

The sequence of events is as follows:

1. **You have a feeling** – happiness, sadness, fear, guilt, anger, etc. This feeling can be traced to some part of the body. For example, someone feeling frightened may complain of 'butterflies in the stomach'; a panicky person may feel tightness in the chest.
2. Imagine yourself **going into the feeling**, being inside your body where the feeling resides.
3. Imagine **what the feeling would look like**.
   In this way you see a representation of the feeling in a visual form.

   Hence the person with 'butterflies in the stomach' may actually imagine something fluttering around in her stomach causing the feeling; the panicky tightness in the chest may look like a rope with a knot pulled tight.

4. The next step is to stay inside the feeling and note any other aspect to the picture – sounds, temperature, heaviness or lightness, movement, associated memories.

   All these observations are *inside the feeling*, not related to reality or logic. This is an imaginary process similar to a dream and dreams are generally not logical by every day standards.

5. When you know all about the feeling you can start to decide if you would like to improve it, alter it, reduce it or change it in any way.

   This can be done by altering any of the components discussed in point 4. The concept is similar to the fact that changing the colour of the sky from grey to blue will change the picture.

6. This alteration of components will lead to an alteration in the emotion. So it is possible to change a shy, self-conscious feeling into a more confident one.

   This process is not straightforward and you will be led in different directions as you proceed. The only real limitation is your creativity and ability to be flexible and think of different alternatives.

Some clinical examples will illustrate the process.

Delia is a 25-year-old art student. She came to see me because she was panicking, believing she couldn't get enough air into her lungs. She was constantly trying to take deeper breaths and becoming more and more anxious as time went by.

She had seen her GP and tests showed her lungs were completely normal – the amount of air she was breathing was completely satisfactory.

The doctor's reassurance had no effect on Delia and he referred her to me.

'How would you describe the feeling you have when you can't get enough air, Delia?'

'It's really frightening. I feel really panicky like I'm going to die.'

'Where abouts in your body is this feeling?'

'In my chest it feels tight and constricted.'

'I'd like you to do something quite strange. I'd like you to close your eyes and imagine you are inside your chest next to that feeling. I'd like you to tell me what it looks like.'

Delia closed her eyes and sat quietly for a minute or two.

'It's dark and I can just see myself lying down. I look very pale and I'm not breathing. Its very scary, perhaps I'm dead.'

'No wonder you feel panicky with pictures like that in your chest. How do you think that picture got there?'

'I have no idea. I don't like it, it makes me feel all creepy.'

'Something is projecting that picture in your chest, look behind you and see if you can see the projector.'

'Yes, I can.'

'Go back to the projector and see who is running it.'

'There is a nasty looking man there.'

'Ask him why he is showing such awful pictures.'

'He says because I've been bad.'

'What would you like to do with the man and those pictures?'

'I'd like to get rid of him and have someone else run the projector showing healthy pictures.'

'All right, do that now. Take your time and let me know when you have made the change.'

Delia sat quietly with her eyes closed for about five minutes then smiled a little.

'It's done. He's gone and a friend of mine is running the projector. He's agreed to show healthy pictures in my chest, pictures that correspond to the doctor's reports and the tests.'

'Good. When you are ready keep that good healthy feeling and open your eyes.'

Delia gradually opened her eyes and stretched.

'That was amazing. I could really see those things. I feel a bit foolish talking about strange men in my chest. Who was that nasty little man?'

'I really don't know and as long as he has been replaced by someone more suitable it really doesn't matter. I would like you to spend 10 minutes every night before you go to bed quietly checking that the new projectionist is still operating the projector, showing you healthy suitable pictures. I'll see you in two weeks time.'

Delia cancelled her next appointment as she said she was feeling really well. She had not had any more panic attacks and all was well with the pictures in her chest.

Barry is 10 years old. Two years ago, since his parents split up, he has been spending every second weekend with his father. Over the last two months he had become very unhappy, cried a lot and wanted to stay with his father *every* weekend.

His mother came to see me concerned about the change in Barry and explained that owing to various circumstances, it was not possible for Barry to stay with his father every weekend.

IMAGINE WHAT THE FEELING WOULD BE LIKE...

I talked to Barry and listened to his concerns. He cried as he talked about having to leave his Dad. He was not sure why the change in his feeling had happened.

'How do you feel when you leave Dad?' I asked him.

'I feel really sad,' he said, as tears welled up.

'Whereabouts is this sadness? Where in your body?'

He indicated his stomach.

'Could you go in there for me and tell me what you see?'

'I see a sad picture. I see me feeling very sad because I'm leaving Dad and I miss him.'

'Your mum had told me it is not possible for you to visit every weekend, so as second best would you like to make the feeling better?'

'Yes, please. I don't like this feeling. I don't like crying; it upsets Mum too and it spoils the time I have with Dad.'

'Would you like to put a happy picture there instead?'

'Yes.'

'Can you think of one that would help your feelings?'

'I think I'll put in a picture of me seeing Dad again in two weeks time.'

'That sounds good. Let me know when that picture is there.'

It didn't take long for Barry to replace the sad picture with a happy one. I asked him to make sure the happy one was there all the time and I would see him in a month.

When I saw Barry again he was much better. His Mum reported he had changed remarkably. He looked forward to seeing his Dad and there were no more scenes or nagging to go every weekend. Barry didn't want to tell his Mum about the pictures in his tummy; she said, whatever we had done, it had worked miracles.

People with low self-confidence often have difficulty making decisions. There are many reasons for this: they don't think of their needs, are concerned what others will think, are frightened of making mistakes and 'raise the plank' so that the importance of the decision is exaggerated.

Many clients say, 'If I don't know what I want, how can I make a decision what to do?' Fear and anxiety fuel the difficulties and sometimes they are unable to decide even the most trivial things: 'Should I have tea or coffee? Should I go to the hairdressers today or tomorrow?'

A visualisation technique that has proved useful is the 'pathways technique'. The steps involved are as follows:

1. Sit quietly with your eyes closed.
2. Imagine you are walking along a lovely pathway in the country.
3. Imagine you come to a crossroads where the path splits into a number of paths. (The number equals the number of choices involved in the decision-making).
4. Imagine going down the first path (which represents one of the choices) into the future for a period of time (days, weeks, months or years depending upon the decision involved).
5. Experience the experiences you will have by making this choice.
6. When you have reached the time ahead, leave that person (the one who makes this choice) there and come back to the crossroads.
7. Go down the next path (a second choice) in a similar manner experiencing what will happen if you make this choice.
8. Leave that person there and if there are more choices, choose more pathways.
9. When you have completed the choices stay at the cross-roads and look at the 'future you' on each path.
10. Choose which 'future you' you would like to be and use this pathway to get there.

Realise if there are two choices A and B then you have three options:

1. Decide to do A
2. Decide to do B
3. Decide not to decide for the time being.

Terence was a young lawyer of 26 working for a law firm. He was unhappy there but had been promised a future position in the firm with economic security.

'I really don't know what to do. I'm married with a young child. If I leave and go to the country, which is what I would like, I may become bored and I certainly wouldn't earn as much. In my present firm I have a guarantee. If I leave I'm taking a risk. I really don't know what to do.'

I discussed the decision-making technique with Terence and he agreed to try it.

'Just close your eyes and relax for a minute or so. When you are ready imagine you are walking along a lovely country path. When you can see that in your mind's eye nod your head.'

Terence nodded his head.

'Now imagine the path continues straight ahead – indicating staying in the present job, and also a branch goes to the right. Imagine you are continuing on the path straight ahead for the next 10 years and when you reach 36 nod your head.'

When Terence nodded his head, I said, 'Good, leave that Terence there and go back to the crossroad. This time take the right-hand road, the one that represents a move to the country. Stay on that road for 10 years experiencing what would happen if you made that choice. When you reach 36 on this road nod your head.'

After a little while he nodded his head again.

'Good, leave that Terence there and go back to the crossroad. Look ahead to the two Terences, the one straight ahead staying at the London firm and the one on the right moving to the country. Observe them both for a little while noting what you see and how you feel. When you are ready, allow yourself to slowly come back into the room and open your eyes.'

After a little while Terence opened his eyes and said, 'That was great. I really saw it clearly. The one straight ahead looked most unhappy. He had a big house but was working all the time. The one on the right was sitting by the fire laughing. He had children all around him and seemed very happy. He felt so much better than the other one.'

'Good. What I suggest is you add that to all the other information you have gathered to help you with the decision.'

Terence *did* decide to move to the country. He is happy there and feels he made the right choice. If he is in London on business he sometimes drops in to see me and says he can't wait to get back to the country.

The changing of feelings into pictures is not a difficult task. It requires quiet time, an attitude of allowing it to happen rather than making it happen, the ability to suspend belief and accept whatever weird and wonderful pictures may appear, and the creativity to alter the pictures to ones that will produce better feelings.

The internal pictures are sometimes scenes, people, colours, shapes tunnels, drawings, etc. The value lies in accepting whatever appears. Creativity is important as is letting go of logic and control.

A slight change in your emotional kaleidoscope will produce a greater appreciation of the external world.

CONFIDENCE BOOSTERS

- Our senses tell us what is happening inside and outside our bodies. Two of these senses are feeling and sight. It is possible to convert one to the other – seeing something wonderful is converted into a feeling of happiness. We are also able to do the reverse – convert a feeling into a picture. This is called creative visualisation.

  Sit quietly with your eyes closed and recall a pleasant feeling that has happened recently.

  Note where the feeling is in your body and allow the mind to convert it into a picture. What does the feeling look like?

  Do this with a number of feelings both positive and negative so you begin to learn about your 'emotional map'.

- Choose an unpleasant emotion you have recently had then choose an emotion which you would enjoy more in that situation. For example, I felt agitated when someone who said they would ring back failed to do so. I would rather have felt calm.

  Repeat the exercise above to locate and visualise those two feelings. Enlarge the positive picture and reduce the negative one.

  Imagine the situation happening again, this time with the large positive picture representing the feeling you would prefer.

  Keep repeating this exercise until a habit pattern is formed where the enjoyable feeling occurs as a response to the situation.

26

Our Inner Worlds

Whenever we receive information or have an experience we process it in four stages:

1. **The experience itself** This can be external or an internal thought or emotion.
2. **Our inner world** This is a complex structure composed of memories, thoughts, feelings, instincts, energy, internal pictures and words, belief systems and analytic processes.
3. **An internal response** This is in the form of a thought, feeling, decision.
4. **An external reaction** This involves an outcome of behaviour or attitude.

This sequence of events occurs very quickly and is generally beyond our conscious awareness until the external reaction 4. occurs.

The most crucial part of this process is 2. 'Our inner world' as this dictates the outcome. It *interprets* the experience in much the same way that a tightly knit community responds to an outsider. The community may greet him as a friend, entertain him as a guest or reject him as an intruder.

Someone who has had many traumatic experiences in the past may well develop an inner world that is protective and focused on survival. Such a complex would contain advice urging caution and avoidance. The internal dialogue may be: 'Don't do that; be wary of this; watch out for him; be careful of going there, etc.'

Any information reaching such an inner world would be directed by caution, fear and worry.

If, however, past experiences were positive and successful, an inner world would develop containing supportive exploratory comments and confident feelings which would result in a 'have-a-go' attitude.

Our inner world is actually divided into many inner worlds; each tailored to respond to specific situations. Some are more helpful than others and it is important that we direct experiences through these more successful worlds so that we can deal with them in more appropriate ways.

If we are struggling to cope in a specific area of our lives, we can bring in strengths that have proven to be helpful in another area.

If we represent the sequence of events:

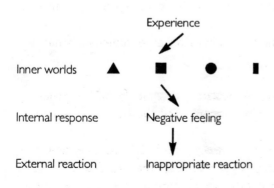

We may be able to alter the sequence to:

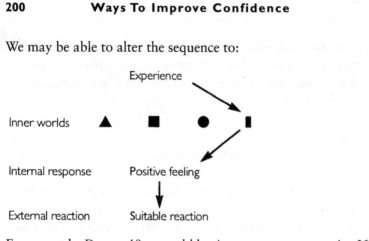

For example, Don, a 40-year-old businessman was a worrier. He dealt with experiences this way:

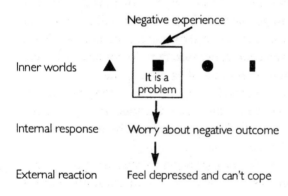

After discussing alternatives Don put time and effort into improving his response:

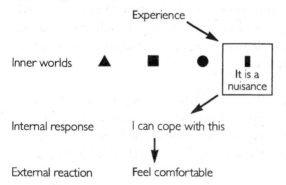

Don had the knowledge already, he just needed help to move his processing mechanism from the inner world of 'worry about problems' to the inner world of 'it's only a nuisance' and the outcome was greatly improved.

The Sausage Machine

Some people appear to only have one form of inner world, one way to interpret the facts that confront them. I refer to such people as having 'a sausage machine' type of inner world. This is because whatever experience they have, the result is the same.

We could compare this to the preparation of a meal. If all that is available is a sausage machine then sausages will be the result whether the initial ingredients are fillet steak or mutton. With sausage machine-type people, because they do not have a variety of inner worlds, their response is always the same.

If guilt is the main internal component then they find themselves guilty irrespective of the circumstances. If anger is the main feature then they find some reason to be angry, even if everything appears to be running smoothly.

As life has a multitude of experiences to offer us, having only one inner world makes it difficult for us to enjoy the variety available.

For most of us there are many inner worlds, each processing information in a slightly different way because of different components making up the complex structure of each inner world. What is important is that the processing structure is suitable for the information received.

Jeremy was in his 40s, he worked as a computer operator in a small firm. His childhood was dominated by a critical and oppressive father. He came to seek my help for problems with panic attacks whenever he had to deal with his boss at work.

Jeremy told me he felt really comfortable in the presence of his friends and workmates, but when he came into contact with an authority figure he panicked.

I discussed the concept of the inner world with him and asked him to draw a diagram of two of his worlds – one when he was with his friends and workmates and the other when he was with his boss. He came to the next session with the following diagrams:

With friends and workmates the sequence was:	With my boss the sequence was:
Experience I am with them having lunch ↓	**Experience** I am in the boss's office and he is talking to me ↓
My inner world consists of:	**My inner world consists of:**
pictures – I can see myself happy and relaxed *words* – I tell myself, 'These are my friends and they like me'. *feelings* – comfortable and relaxed feeling in my chest	*feeling* – I feel I am out of control; I feel a tremor and tension in my stomach, a little like when I was young *words* – I tell myself not to make a fool of myself as he'll get angry. I ask myself, 'Am I in trouble; have I done something wrong?' Sometimes I get flashbacks from past experiences when I was frightened and not in control
↓	↓
Internal response I feel good all over ↓	**Internal response** Fear and panic in my stomach ↓
External reaction I have a confident attitude and behave in a relaxed, natural way. I feel this is the real me.	**External reaction** I panic and words don't come out of my mouth properly. I dry up and don't say what I would like to say. I have complete loss of confidence.

Jeremy and I discussed these two inner worlds, how they had come about and how he could improve his response to his boss. He told me his boss was a pleasant man and had never treated him badly so he couldn't understand why he panicked so much in his presence.

We agreed he had a strong and positive inner world when dealing with his friends and thought about ways he could use this ability to deal with his boss. He realised it was the way he *perceived* the experience that determined which inner world would process it.

The conclusion Jeremy reached was that if he could change the perspective of his boss from 'authority figure' to 'friend' then the inner world used to process his experiences would change from the second to the first.

'I don't think I can do that,' he said thoughtfully. 'How can I regard my boss as a friend?'

'I would have thought that was possible', I replied. 'Over the next few weeks focus on the humane aspects of him, think of him as a family man, how he potters around the house and does what your other friends do at home. Recall the times he has been nice to you – friendly. Build up a library of pictures and words that depict him as a normal man such as yourself.'

Over the following weeks Jeremy built up an 'identikit' image of his boss as a normal human being and as he did so his panics subsided. Over a period of time the processing mechanism changed from:

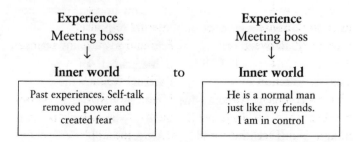

Experience		Experience
Meeting boss		Meeting boss
↓		↓
Inner world	to	**Inner world**
Past experiences. Self-talk removed power and created fear		He is a normal man just like my friends. I am in control

Six months later I received a letter saying he had been able to have lunch with his boss and felt just the same as he did with his friends.

We have the tools to deal with most situations but often don't have access to these tools.

Some people are caged in an inner world of shouldn't, fear, guilt or worry and are restricted by these caging elements, unable to use positive worlds that could serve them more successfully. As experiences are diverted to the cage they become enmeshed in negativity with disastrous outcomes.

On the other hand, confident people have inner worlds that provide all the necessary thoughts and emotions to create that confidence. Even if mistakes happen and failures occur, the inner world is able to bolster the person so that confidence in themselves remains intact.

In a way their inner world is acting as a best friend (see Chapter 27 How to be Your Own Best Friend), providing support and understanding to help them through the highs and lows that naturally occur in life. Challenges are met with help and encouragement from within. A pattern develops which is put into practice when the situation requires it.

A friend of mine who has had many tragedies in his life still has his optimism and confidence. He explained to me that his attitude was: 'If something goes wrong in my life, I say to myself it is due to *external* factors. If something goes right I tell myself that was due to *me*.'

Rosie had a very positive outlook on life. She was generally happy, coping well with her three children, job and busy husband. She came to see me to stop smoking and our discussion wandered on to her inner worlds.

When we analysed them she described encouraging, positive words, pictures and feelings that created an optimistic response to the majority of events occurring in her life.

'If something goes wrong, one of the children is sick, I imagine what it will be like when he is better,' she remarked as she thought about her inner world. 'It is lovely and bright in there, it feels good and I remember lots of happy times and people. I had a really good childhood: Mum and Dad were great parents to my brother and myself.'

'How do you think your inner world deals with things?' I asked.

She thought for a while and looked at the ceiling.

'It's a great help to me, like a friend it gives me good advice, it's balanced I suppose and sees the good side of things and people.'

'Do you ever get down or depressed?'

'Oh, I certainly do, but I know it won't last. It is as if I'm in a tunnel but I can see the light at the end so it's not so bad. And it always turns out all right. My husband is very helpful and we talk a lot about any problems that arise.'

'How is it you are not able to give up smoking?'

'I really don't know. It's the one thing that bothers me, it's out of my control and I feel bad about it. I worry how it will affect the children and so does my husband. But I know you'll be able to help me.'

'Would it be all right if we used hypnosis to help your inner world stop you smoking?'

She smiled. 'Yes, that would be really good, I need something. I know I can do it but I just need something to help me.'

'All right, close your eyes and take a little while to relax, focus on your breathing and feel yourself drifting into the inner world that helps you solve problems and overcome hurdles.'

I then went through a hypnotic procedure to help Rosie go into a deep state of relaxation.

'Now that you are fully relaxed I'd like you to choose some parts of your inner world that would help you be a non-smoker, a free-breather. Parts that will positively encourage you and point out to you that you already have that ability, as that was how you were for the first 16 years of your life. Wander into your lungs and realise how they will feel when they are breathing fresh air rather than smoke, tar and nicotine. Be aware that your lungs are your friends and they work hard a thousand times a day to keep you healthy. See yourself and your family living in a healthy smoke-free zone and experience the good feeling of not feeling guilty and hiding things from the children. Use your positive inner world to process these things and help you back to being a free-breather.'

Rosie sat quietly with her eyes closed and an attitude of focused inner attention for about twenty minutes. She was doing her own work and didn't need my interference.

I quietly said, 'When you know, and every part of you knows you will be a free-breather from now on please nod your head.'

She slowly nodded her head.

'When you are ready, slowly and comfortably drift back into the room and open your eyes.'

She remained motionless for a few minutes then gradually opened her eyes and stretched. She smiled and said, 'That was just great. I actually saw my inner world – it was bright and cheery and full of colours. I saw my lungs caked black with tar – disgusting – and felt really strongly it was time to stop poisoning them. Somehow I know I will do it and it may not be as difficult as I imagined. One of the messages I was getting was 'Now is the time to do it.'

Rosie did stop smoking. She used her positive inner world to make the transition from smoker to free-breather in a manner much easier than most. Her positive attitude and confidence that things turn out for the best helped her with a difficult task.

We can use the concept of our inner worlds to learn how we process our experiences. Having the ability to deal with some things means it may be possible to use this ability to deal with other things using a similar process.

Often when I see clients and we discuss their problems and how to deal with them more successfully they say, 'I actually knew that but I didn't actually realise I knew it.'

These people are gaining access to internal worlds that were already working for them in other areas of their lives.

Things are neither good nor bad
But thinking makes them so.

SHAKESPEARE

CONFIDENCE BOOSTERS

- The concept of inner worlds describes how we process experiences, either external, or internal ones like thoughts or feelings. The inner world is complex, consisting of memories, words, thoughts, instinct, etc.

  Choose an experience that happens repeatedly such as going to work or eating a meal. Think of the internal components involved that create the external reaction – thoughts, feelings, past experiences. In this way you are beginning to become aware of your 'processing mechanism' – the way you deal with simple repetitive experiences.

- Choose a situation where the external reaction is inappropriate to the situation; i.e. the bus is late and you fume and swear.

  Choose another situation where your method of coping is satisfactory: i.e. your boss is late and you accept it.

  Now study the inner worlds involved and devise ways of altering pictures, changing words, improving perspectives (See Chapter 23 Walking the Plank) to convert the first situation into the second response.

  Do this with a variety of situations where you would like to improve your coping mechanism.

27

How to be Your Own
Best Friend

I was talking to a friend about things that had helped her improve her confidence. She said the most important thing she can remember was when aged 19 (she is now 35), she was feeling low after a broken relationship and realised she was talking to herself as two people an '*I*' and a '*me*'.

'*I* was giving *myself* a hard time. *I* was blaming *myself* for what had happened and being judgemental, critical and punishing to *myself*.

I realised I would never behave like this to any of my friends and it suddenly dawned on me – from now on, *I'm going to be my own best friend*.'

And she was; and has been ever since with amazing results.

'I am happier, easier to get on with. I've been more successful and good things have happened to me. Life is much less of a struggle as I'm there to give myself support through the difficult times.'

There are a few unchangeable facts about adult life.

1. We need to accept responsibility for our actions.
2. Our actions and attitudes have outcomes.

This does not mean we *cause* all our difficulties, but we need to accept responsibility for them so we can change them if we wish.

I often ask my clients:

Q. 'Who is the most important person to you?'
A. 'My wife.'
Q. 'And next?'
A. 'My children.'
Q. 'And next?'
A. 'My parents.'
Q. 'And next?'
A. 'My best friend.'

At this stage I say, 'And what about yourself?' They look at me in a strange way and say, 'Oh. I didn't know you meant me. I never thought of that. I'd forgotten all about me.'

'Yes. That's exactly why I asked the question. You are constantly forgetting about yourself. That's the reason you are having so many difficulties.'

You are the most important person in your life. You have to live with yourself till you die. Others may come and go but you will remain with yourself till the end.

If you treat yourself badly, as an inferior, of no worth, then this journey called life is going to be that much more difficult. If you treat yourself as a friend your journey will be more pleasant and rewarding.

Many readers may be saying, 'But that is so selfish. I was brought up to be modest and self-effacing. I was told it was swollen-headed and egotistical to put myself first. I was told I wouldn't be liked if I did things like that.' (See Chapter 28 In Praise of Being Selfish.) I agree there needs to be a balance. But when clients regard their dog as more important than themselves I believe the balance is tilted too far away from the optimum.

Being your own best friend is easy and difficult at the same time. Easy because you know how to do it, difficult because it requires effort to change old habits.

ALL YOU NEED IS TO BEHAVE TOWARDS YOURSELF EXACTLY AS YOU WOULD TOWARDS YOUR BEST FRIEND.

All you need to do is behave towards yourself exactly as you would behave towards your best friend if they were in your situation. That's it in a nutshell!

If you would value them and their needs, then do the same to yourself. If you would care and support them in troubled times, then do the same to yourself. If you would praise and congratulate them on their success then . . . etc.

To do this you need to give yourself an essential commodity – *quality time*; time for you to reflect and treat yourself as a friend. Just as you need to spend quality time with your friend.

It's all so simple really. There is nothing complicated about what I am suggesting. There is no need to look for risks, problems or hidden agendas. There are only two requirements:

1. The decision to be your best friend.
2. Just doing it.

One practical way of learning to be your own best friend is called 'mirror work'.

Whenever you look in the mirror spend a little time 'talking to yourself'. The form of this talking should be praising, liking, admiring the 'you in the mirror'.

Learn to 'look yourself in the face' and talk as a friend to the image you see. Use encouraging words about the day ahead or complimentary words about the previous 24 hours.

In this way you are imitating positive self-talk that will be continued throughout the day. Make good use of the time when you need to look in the mirror or allow five minutes a day just to talk to your mirrored friend.

Let's go back to the two points I mentioned earlier:

1. Our actions and attitudes have outcomes.
2. We need to accept responsibility for these outcomes.

Imagine the journeys through life of two different people.

Jim loathes himself and is constantly giving himself a hard time. Percy is his own best friend.

The outcomes, in similar situations, for these two men will be vastly different. The barriers and hurdles Jim erects by his attitude makes his journey so much more difficult than that of Percy.

Percy is accompanied by a friend to share experiences with. Jim is accompanied by an enemy and they continue their journey in angry silence.

Many clients say to me 'I'm my own worst enemy' and they are correct in that assessment of themselves. Wouldn't it be preferable to travel through life with your best friend rather than your worst enemy?

The only way to have a friend is to be one.
RALPH WALDO EMERSON

CONFIDENCE BOOSTERS

- If we treat ourselves as our own best friend the journey through life would be so much easier and happier. Often this is not the case and we call ourselves negative critical names.

  Think about your best friend, have the feeling you have when asked by them for a favour. Compare that with your attitude towards yourself. How would you go about improving the way you feel towards yourself, your response when mistakes occur?
- There are two rules for adult behaviour:
  - Our actions and attitudes have outcomes.
  - We need to accept responsibility for these outcomes.

  Think about these two points in relation to outcomes that have happened to you recently. Are you able to accept the responsibility or did you blame it on others?

Do you believe these two rules play a part in your attitude towards yourself? If you are hard on yourself, does this have a negative outcome that you take responsibility for?
- Would you describe your attitude as:
  - treating yourself as a friend?
  - hard on yourself?
  - having a self-destructive tendency?
  - putting yourself down with blame and criticism?

28

In Praise of Being Selfish

'Suzannah, you are very stressed. You have been working too hard and need time for yourself. I will give you a relaxation tape and would like you to have an hour a day for yourself.'

'Doctor, I couldn't do that. That would be too selfish!'

I hear this comment every day when I suggest people take time for themselves. The stigma of being selfish blocks any opportunity for a balanced life. Selfish people are nasty, unpopular and basically bad.

Well, I disagree. I believe being selfish is a good thing. The dictionary definition is 'chiefly concerned with one's own interest'. I think that is a very healthy attitude and in some strange way is linked to confidence.

When you are confident you have the ability to be concerned with your own interest and not feel ashamed of it.

I am not talking about the selfish person who eats the last two pieces of cake. I believe there is a healthy balance between looking after yourself and being aware of the needs of others. There is a spectrum between the martyr – never being assertive, always thinking of others, believing he has no rights and must not upset anyone – and the self-opinionated egocentric person who *only* thinks of his own needs.

I believe selfish comes somewhere in the middle. The word has received very bad press over the years and perhaps more so in Britain than other countries. I would like to apply for the honorary role of being its PR agent.

I think looking after yourself is a very healthy attitude. To have an hour a day to relax and allow the bodily systems to recover is in everyone's best interest.

> Ashley saw me for burnout (overwork), and was reluctant to have time to relax. He said not doing anything was a waste. I insisted he sat quietly for 20 minutes a day. He returned the next week looking very sheepish.
>
> 'My wife won't let me lie down for half an hour. She says I'm being selfish and should help with things around the house.'
>
> We discussed this and I asked 'Would it be of help if I gave you a relaxing tape and you can tell her I've requested you to listen to it daily.'
>
> His eyes lit up. 'I think that may work.'
>
> He returned the following week, his face was beaming.
>
> 'My wife has agreed to my listening to the tape because I'm doing something and that is not selfish.'

I believe many people use the words 'I don't want to be selfish' as a smoke screen to hide their lack of confidence. They are overly concerned what others will think. Will they think I'm uncaring? Will they call me selfish behind my back? Will they think I'm unable to cope?

Having the courage to like yourself, be yourself and look after your needs is a healthy attitude. Having the ability to look after others as well is also important. But if your energy has dropped and all you are capable of doing is looking after yourself then that is what you should do. By following this pattern you will build energy and in time be able to look after others as well.

Mothers seem to develop this aversion to selfishness more than fathers. Perhaps having children requires them to devote all their time to the needs of the child. This pattern is then instilled so that focusing on yourself causes guilt. Maternal instinct is so strong that initially the 'self' becomes lost in the child.

Many mothers lose themselves in the needs of their children. Constant demands mean they have less time for themselves, this leads to a belief that they are less important than others.

It is a difficult line to draw between one's own needs as a mother and the needs of the children. Some mothers become martyrs and sacrifice everything for the child's needs.

As the children grow and need the mother less she becomes lost as if abandoned by them. Her aims in life were so inextricably entwined with her children that she suffers greatly as they reach adolescence and develop their own powers.

Often mothers such as these have modelled their lives on *their* mother's or been directed to 'give all' for the children. Discussing selfishness with them falls on deaf ears, they regard their own needs as of no importance and time for themselves is translated as depriving their children.

Often when I struggle to encourage clients to have time for themselves and they resist, they say 'I put myself last, I know I do, but anything for a peaceful life.'

These people have the *least peaceful life of anyone I see*. Their lives are generally in turmoil, they have no control, use avoidance as their main coping strategy and are forever hoping things will get better by themselves.

Changing the word selfish to 'looking after yourself' reduces the guilt. As one of the aims in life is to take responsibility for ourselves, how can we achieve this if we are not concerned with our own interest?

There are a group of people I call 'problem thieves'. They are always on the look out to steal someone's problem from them and try and fix it.

Leonore is a good example.

'My mother worries herself sick about me. I know I'm 35 but she can't stop worrying. I ring her three times a day to reassure her I'm all right but it doesn't seem to help.'

'Whose problem is it?'

'Why, I suppose it's hers, but I feel I should be responsible. She *is* worrying about me, so I think I should fix it.'

'Whose problem is it?'

'My mother's. I know it's hers but . . .'

'Whose problem is it? If it is your mother's problem, why are you trying to steal it from her. You used to ring her once a day. That didn't solve it. You then rang her twice a day. That didn't solve it. Now you are ringing her three times a day and she still is anxious about you.'

'But it would be selfish if I didn't care.'

'I'm not suggesting you don't care. I'm suggesting you care enough about your mother to let her deal with her own problems.'

No one can fix another's problem. You can help them solve it but you can't fix it for them. If the daughter discussed 'the problem' with her mother in a caring and supportive way, the merry-go-round of phone calls may not escalate.

The mother, too, is a thief, she is 'stealing' her daughter's right to her own life. By constantly reminding her how much she is worrying she is transferring her daughter's problems to herself without any attempt to help her resolve them. She is not acting in a supportive role, and in a way is 'stealing the worry'. This in fact compounds the problem rather than easing it.

Strange though it may seem 'selfish' people are often popular; they give off vibrations that they know who they are and what they want. They are not dependent on the opinion of others for their survival.

Those with low self-esteem, who do not like themselves, require the approval of others for their survival. They believe they will achieve this approval by giving, by being unselfish.

In life this is not the case, this attitude radiates vibrations that something false is happening. People picking up these vibrations do not respond by closeness, love and support, but by distancing themselves as the messages are not straight but distorted by need.

Unfortunately those who so desperately need support and closeness do not receive it. If only they would risk being selfish – being themselves – the result may be far more positive.

Too often our behaviour is dictated by obligation to others, in the process we forget the primary obligation – to be ourselves.

CONFIDENCE BOOSTERS

- Most people feel the word selfish is very negative and would not like to have the term applied to themselves. It is possible to reframe it as 'focusing on your own needs' and thus having a much more acceptable meaning.

  What is your attitude to the word 'selfish'? Can you appreciate how it may be beneficial for you to become more selfish?

- 'What will people think if I do that?' is a common phrase I hear from people who lack confidence. Is this something you tell yourself to avoid actions? Replace 'What will people think?' with 'People think about themselves.' And notice the effect on your attitude. The reality is that in general people do not notice and so it is a more appropriate phrase to have in your mind.

29

Confidence in Relationships

Imagine a cog. This is a very special cog that has five basic components.

1. The number of spines
2. The different length of each spine
3. The space between the spines
4. The rate at which it is rotating
5. The direction in which it is rotating.

Demonstrated diagramatically it may look like this:

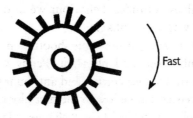

This cog is a representation of a man called Tom. The spaces, lengths and rate have all built up over the years. The original spines have altered – some have grown, others have worn down. This cog is like a fingerprint of Tom; it embodies all his characteristics. It is a complex cog made up of likes, dislikes, attitudes, strengths, weaknesses, beliefs, etc. It is one way of knowing Tom.

Some months ago Tom met Penny. He found her very attractive and they started a relationship.

Penny's cog looks like this.

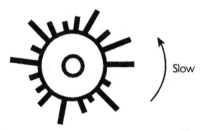

As Tom and Penny went out together their cogs got closer. The dating, chatting, expressing feelings, sex, discussions all cause the rotating cogs to begin to enmesh.

You can well imagine the outcome! Not only are the spines of different length and space but the cogs are rotating in different directions and at different speeds.

You may say that such people would never get together or be attracted to each other. This is not so. There are many relationships that have differences similar to Tom and Penny and it is not surprising when things start to go wrong in the relationship. Their values, attitudes, behaviour were so very different that harmony was most unlikely.

Tom was a 'huntin', fishin' and shootin'' man who loved rare beef, lamb chops and pheasant. Penny was an animal rights worker, staunch vegetarian and anti-hunt protester.

These differences can be lost in the first bloom of love. The sentence 'he will change' or 'she will change', plays non-stop in a tape-recording in their minds! Inevitably, in time, their true self comes through and the relationship fails. It is too difficult to maintain individual identities and also respect those of one's partner.

Confidence in a relationship requires:

Confidence in yourself

Liking yourself is important if you are going to like someone else. How can you expect her to like you if you don't value yourself?

The psychiatrist R.D. Laing put it succinctly:

'I don't like myself because I'm worthless.
Suzie likes me.
Suzie must be hopeless to like someone as worthless as me.
How could I like Suzie if she as is hopeless as that.'

Or as Groucho Marx said:

'I would never join a club that would have me as a member.'

Many people who have a low opinion of themselves enter a relationship in the hope that their partner will make things better by their love and praise. It doesn't work. You can never get enough praise from others to replenish your diminished self-esteem. Their praise vanishes like the mist and you need more and more until you drive your partner away in frustration.

This then completes the self-fulfilling prophecy. When your partner leaves it is proof you are no good, reinforcing your initial belief. As Louise Hay states, everything that comes to us is either:

a) what we give out or   b) what we think we deserve

Love your partner as he/she is

So often couples going through the traumas of separation say, 'I thought I could change him/her.' As a basic rule people don't change due to pressure from others. They may alter a little on the surface but their main character remains the same.

Unconditional love is just what it says, loving without conditions. In my experience it is a rare commodity. It is more common to let our own values and opinions interfere with the feelings about our partner.

One of the basic flaws in relationships is mistaking 'she is different' for 'she is wrong'. We use our own values to judge our partner and when there is a difference we label her as wrong rather than appreciating the difference.

Another way of stating this is:

- Each partner has a different attitude, belief system and behaviour pattern.
- One or both partners are not able to *respect* the attitude of the other.
- Judgements, arguments, blame and criticism follow.

In many cases it is very difficult to respect an attitude and behaviour which is very different to one's own beliefs. Working on this respect and acceptance may well have more benefit than trying to change the other partner.

A relationship could be described as having each partners' needs met. He has needs of her and she has needs of him.

Many people have no idea of the needs of their partner. How could they fulfil these needs if they don't know what they are?

Relationships are often full of 'shoulds', rather than being open to each other's needs. It may be that you cannot fulfil your partner's needs but being aware of them and discussing them allows a closeness to develop.

Perhaps the problems arise because of our original choice of partner. This choice ignores what we know on an intuitive, gut level. We hope/believe things will be different, will change. Generally our basic intuition is proved to be correct with the passage of time.

To have confidence in your own intuition when choosing a partner

Often when I see partners splitting up I ask why they are splitting up.

They describe the 'faults' that are causing the breakdown. I ask them when they *first* knew about these faults. They think for a while and generally say 'The first week we went out together. I knew at a deep level it wasn't right but I ignored that feeling because we were having such a good time.'

Having confidence in that 'deep down' feeling helps us make a more suitable choice for a long-term relationship.

The confidence to be yourself

Some years ago, a doctor friend came to stay. His wife was away and we were attending a seminar together.

In the morning I asked him if he wanted Weetabix for breakfast. 'Weetabix. Don't offer me bloody Weetabix. I hate the stuff,' he exclaimed with great emotion. 'Hold on a minute,' I said, surprised by his outburst, 'all I did was offer you breakfast. There was no need to fly off the handle.'

He regained his composure. 'I'm terribly sorry. I lost my head for a minute and forgot myself. It was a reflex reaction. I got married 10 years ago. We had a wonderful honeymoon in Barbados. On the first morning my new wife said to me at breakfast, 'Don't you just love Weetabix?' Like a fool I agreed and have been eating it ever since and I hate the stuff. I can't tell her now as she'll know I've been lying all the time.'

My friend was unable to be himself in that aspect of his relationship. Because he tried to please his wife on the first day, he had maintained that attitude ever since and his pent up emotion was demonstrated at my breakfast table.

Trying to contort your 'real self' to fit with your partner's expectations is like wearing shoes that are too small. Eventually problems arise. Some degree of moulding occurs during a relationship but not being free to be yourself puts a great deal of strain on yourself and your partner.

Being yourself *does* take confidence. A little voice in the back of the mind whispers (or shouts), 'What if she doesn't like you if you do that' and so avoidance seems the preferable action.

We all have a dark side, a shadow. Accepting, acknowledging

and expressing this part of ourselves takes away it's power. By denying and avoiding it we keep it in the darkness where, like fungus, it grows profusely.

When I ask clients about being themselves, many reply 'I really don't know who I am'. They have played a role in life rather than being themselves so have lost touch with who they are. If you don't know who you are it will be difficult for your partner to find out.

The confidence to listen

I believe one of the major problems in communication is that so few people actually listen to what others are saying.

Communication means the sending of messages from one person to another in such a way that the second person receives and acknowledges the message.

This requires:

* attentive listening in order to hear what is being said.
* a pause for a few seconds to let the speaker know he has been heard – 'the essential pause'
* a response

In my experience many people are so involved in their own thoughts, and their reply, that they are not focused on the message – they are not listening. The 'essential pause' is often missing and the speaker does not feel listened to (because he isn't). I say confidence is required to be a good listener and that is true. The insecure person is having an internal dialogue 'I hope he doesn't find out how dumb I am. I'd better think of a suitable response.' He then thinks of a good reply and has to keep repeating it in his mind in case he forgets it. By doing so he misses the latter part of what the speaker has said and rushes in with his reply ignoring 'the essential pause'.

This causes the speaker to be hurt and feel unheard, and the smooth running of communication disintegrates into anger and distance.

Many people want to talk, few to listen. Having the confidence to be an attentive listener is a great attribute in a relationship. Some say being understood is like being loved.

Confidence to express your expectations

When a relationship begins and throughout the relationship, each partner has expectations of the other. They may not be aware what these needs actually are but they are present at all levels of the mind, body and soul.

Being confident enough to share these expectations with each other puts the relationship on a sound footing. Many people who are insecure do not have the confidence to do this in case rejection results.

Making a list of your expectations may sound too formal, but not allowing your partner to know what you need makes it difficult for them to fulfil your requirements.

Naomi and Douglas came to see me when their relationship was 'falling apart'. They had been together for two years but the love and companionship had been replaced by hostility and arguments.

'What did you expect from Douglas?' I asked a tearful Naomi.

'I hoped he would always be there for me. I hoped he would devote his love and time for me so I could feel secure for once in my life.'

'And what did you expect from Naomi?' I asked an angry Douglas.

'Freedom. I wanted to be free to do what I wished and come home to her for support and love in the home. I don't need her and I don't want to be needed.'

Had Douglas and Naomi been able to express their needs at the outset of their relationship it would have been obvious they would not be having their expectations met. As these expectations remained unspoken the course had been a downward one for the last two years.

Confidence to be vulnerable

Many people fear rejection. They spend most of their time protecting themselves from being hurt. They build walls to prevent feelings they may have experienced in childhood, where parents were critical or not understanding.

At our core we are very sensitive, easily hurt and feel deep pain when rejected. We do not want to feel those feelings again and guard against anyone getting close to 'the real me'. We protect this sensitive part at all costs especially if we do not trust our partner.

The confidence to be vulnerable is a most important part of any relationship. It is a step-by-step process as layers are removed much like peeling an onion. It allows partners to become closer to each other and requires trust, respect and understanding to proceed.

Too often our hurt throws up a brick wall to protect the sensitive inner self. This creates tension followed by distance. Vulnerability is a strength not a weakness and an essential ingredient for any close relationship.

Listing the confidences involved in relationships:

1. Confidence in yourself.
2. Confidence to love your partner as he/she is.
3. Confidence to follow your gut reaction.
4. Confidence to be yourself.
5. Confidence to be an attentive listener.
6. Confidence to express your expectations.
7. Confidence to be vulnerable.

Being aware of these and focusing your mind on them means you are putting energy into your relationship. This energy is required for the relationship to grow just as a plant requires nourishment to flourish.

In any relationship there are three important components.

1. You
2. Your partner
3. The relationship

All three require time, attention and caring for the relationship to flourish and grow.

---

*Oh, the comfort, the inexpressible comfort, of feeling safe
with a person; having neither to weigh thoughts, nor
measure words, but pour them all out, just as they are, chaff
and grain together, knowing that a faithful hand will take
and sift them, keep what is worth keeping, and then, with a
breath of kindness, blow the rest away.*

ANON

CONFIDENCE BOOSTERS

- A good relationship could be defined as 'Each partner having their needs met.' This concept requires that each person involved knows what their needs are and the feeling between them is such they can share these needs and respond to these needs. Focusing on a relationship involving yourself ask the following questions:
  - Are you aware of your needs in the relationship?
  - Are you able to share these needs with the other person?
  - Do you know what their needs are of you?
  - Are you able to respect their needs?
  - Are your needs and their needs being met by the relationship?
- Considering there are three entities involved in any relationship:
  - You
  - The other person
  - The relationship

  How much time and effort do you put in to 'the relationship' as compared with your needs or their needs?

- There are five requirements involved in building a strong relationship:
  - Confidence in yourself.
  - Accepting your partner as she/he is.
  - Confidence in your intuition.
  - The confidence to be yourself and your partner to be him/herself.
  - The ability to listen attentively to each other.

  Focus on a relationship you are now in or have previously been in, and ask yourself how relevant those five factors are/were to you.

30

Helping Your Children Become Confident

The attitude we have towards our children should be similar to the way we intend to treat ourselves.

The words love, respect, praise, accept, support, all spring to mind.

Many people come for help and at the same time state how concerned they are that their problems, attitude and behaviour will cause difficulties in their children.

'I'm coming to see you about myself but my major worry is the effect I am having on my 10-year-old daughter.'

We are to a large extent a product of our upbringing. The forces that influence us tend to reproduce many aspects of our parents behaviour. We become caught in a repetitive cycle that requires great energy to break.

'I don't want my children to go through what I did when I was a child,' is an oft-repeated saying, yet in spite of all our best intentions that is often what we do.

To break this repetitive cycle we need to spend much time and effort learning about ourselves, the way we work, how parental influences play a role. By becoming aware of these factors we are in a much better position to avoid handing them on to our children.

Often parents go to the opposite extreme and create problems that way.

'We were poor when I was young so I'm going to make sure my children have everything they want.'

By creating excesses to remove the pain of childhood we create different problems for our children.

I do not intend to tell you how to bring up your children. What I can do is pass on information gleaned from listening to troubled parents and children. Learning by others' mistakes can prove useful at times.

A most amazing man called Monty Roberts lives in Nevada, America. He was brought up on a horse ranch and learnt to ride by the age of two. His father was a very cruel man, harsh to Monty and the horses he trained. He rounded up wild mustangs from the desert and 'broke' them so they could be sold for riding.

The method he used was called 'sacking out'. The horse had each of its four legs tied to a stake. A sack was then thrown over its head to frighten it. Whips were used to show who was master. After three weeks of this torture the horse was 'broken' and able to be ridden.

As a child Monty hated the 'sacking out' process and was determined to find a better way to train horses. He rode out to the desert, camped there, and observed behaviour between the mustangs. He learnt their language which he called 'equus'.

By studying their interactions he learnt to behave like a horse and developed techniques to change wild mustangs into calm horses within half an hour. He called this process 'starting' and it was based on an understanding between man and horse. No whips or fear were used.

On the one hand there was a method used by Monty's father which relied on cruelty, whips and fear and took three weeks; on the other Monty's method of 'starting' using kindness and understanding which took half an hour.

Monty's techniques are described in a wonderful book called *The Man Who Listens to Horses* (see Further Reading) and have been adapted all over the world.

Monty's attitude bears some relevance to ways we can help our children become confident. It is obvious that Monty's father would not be seen as a model for bringing up children.

The essence of Monty's method was to understand the horse well enough to encourage it, so that it *chose* to do what he wanted. His father knew what was best for the horse and forced it into submission.

We as parents provide a role model for our children, they receive messages on many different levels. Children, like animals, are sensitive creatures and notice vibrations going on around them.

Too often we as parents 'tell' rather than 'listen'. We know what is right for them and will instil that knowledge at all costs. Monty listened and observed and in that way was able to understand. Too often I hear the phrase 'I just don't understand my children.' How can we assist in their confidence if we don't understand them?

As with everything in life, there is a balance. If we don't provide a framework, a trellis, limits for them to grow, our children will lose direction. If the framework is too binding, too restrictive they will lose their individuality and fail to achieve their potential.

As confidence is a good feeling about ourselves we need to ask the question 'How can we help our children develop a good feeling about themselves?' The answer lies in the saying: *A child is a flame to be kindled not a vessel to be filled.*

By loving, nurturing, supporting, understanding, giving quality time, praising, we provide that kindling to their flame. A lot to ask of us as parents, especially when there are so many other demands on our time.

Problems arise because we have our 'stuff' that interferes with being perfect parents. Our own angers, fears, needs, guilts prevent us being there as the nurturing parent.

I was at a party once talking to a young woman. During the conversation she remarked her baby was born three days ago. In amazement I asked where the baby was.

'Oh. I didn't want to breastfeed as it would interfere with my

A CHILD IS A FLAME TO BE KINDLED,
NOT A VESSEL TO BE FILLED.

social life. The nanny is looking after him and hopefully he will be asleep when we get home. He sleeps at the far end of the house so he won't disturb my sleep.'

Being too critical and judgemental causes lack of confidence as does being over-protective. Mothers' fears are instilled in their children. *Children learn who they are by what they receive in response to what they do.*

It is important to differentiate between the child and his action. This division sometimes becomes blurred and the 'bad action' becomes mistaken for the 'bad child'.

Too often I hear 'You are a hopeless child', 'You are so stupid', 'You are a terrible boy to do that to your brother.'

All these comments are aimed at the child not the action. 'It is a bad *thing* you are doing' is more accurate and less destructive. Describing the action not the child has a much less harmful effect and is far more helpful in bringing about an improvement in behaviour.

Setting boundaries provides the child with some security. Being consistent is essential. Children with inconsistent parenting struggle to make sense of the world. The alcoholic parent who is loving one day and belligerent the next is the most powerful force for low self-esteem.

A list of do's may be:

1. Love and accept your children.
2. Provide stability and security.
3. Give them quality time.
4. Praise and encourage them.
5. Help them to feel worthwhile.
6. Provide suitable limits to help them grow.
7. Listen so you can understand them.

One of the aims of parenthood is to help children become adults so they can join society as successful, happy, confident people. The real world they enter will not be made of the list above, it will be full of people looking after their own needs.

Giving the message that life is wonderful and everyone lives happily ever after may not be the best message to receive as they make the transition from protected child to responsible adult.

You as parents cannot make your child confident. You can provide the means to allow him to *grow* in a confident way, just as you can help a plant to grow from a seed and reach its full potential with beautiful flowers or healthy fruit. If you force the plant to grow more quickly by using hothouse techniques it will not be able to withstand the weather of the real world.

Your child has the potential to be whatever he or she is going to be. As a parent you can act as a caring gardener does to a precious plant – provides support, nutrients, and protection at the same time as allowing it to experience whatever the weather has to offer.

The attitude throughout is one of *balance*. Problems arise when we move to either end of the scale and become too strict or too lenient. Providing a background of love, praise and support allows the child to grow steadily while exploring avenues and taking risks.

In order to be good parents
Here is a rule of thumb,
To help your child gain confidence
Remember to be Fair, Firm and Fun.

Being aware that your child is unique allows you to enjoy their individuality and not try to mould them to a preconceived model. A. S. Neil who ran a school called Summerhill stated, 'Every child has a God in him. Our attempts to mould the child will turn the God into a devil.'

This is an extreme view – one end of the scale and may well be out of balance with society's requirements. Monty's father's attitude was at the other end of the scale, being a responsible parent hovers somewhere between.

Finding something that your child does well and praising them is an important part of parenting. It plants the seed of confidence and self-esteem which grows in so many different directions.

Gael Lindenfield's *Confident Children* goes step by step through the various aspects of confidence building with children.

As every parent knows, bringing up children is not easy. We can all see the fault in other parents, other children. It is not easy to face our own deficiencies, to be aware of the influence we are having in bringing up our own children.

Before I got married I had six theories about bringing up children; Now I have six children and no theories.

JOHN WILMOT
ENGLISH POET 1647–1680

CONFIDENCE BOOSTERS

- Children thrive on praise, support and understanding and are stunted by constant criticism, blame and judgement. A balance needs to be reached where guidelines are fair, firm and fun.

  Think about ways you were treated as a child and the way you treat your children. Is there any similarity; are you repeating the mould formed by your parents?

- Make a conscious effort to be aware of the words you are using when talking with your children. Are they a balance of encouraging, understanding and supportive words, or are you constantly critical and find it difficult to accept them as they are?

- Choose one aspect of your child's behaviour that you are negative about and find ways you can see this behaviour in a positive light in order to praise him/her.

31

Time and Effort

This book has described many methods helpful in building confidence.

The theories, techniques and case histories are all here – tried and tested. They need only two ingredients to be lifted from the pages into your life.

Your Time and Effort

Without these two ingredients they will remain as theories and techniques forever entombed in this book. They will be a conversation piece, something interesting, 'out there' rather than part of your experience.

A proportion of my clients *do* put in time and effort to tackle their problems. These clients have a great deal of success in achieving their aims largely because of this attitude.

It is important to realise that building confidence is an essential part of enjoying life. Making this a priority ensures that you have the best chance of success. If you tell yourself 'I must do that one day', that day will never come.

There is a saying which illustrates what I mean.

I hear
   – and forget

I see
– and remember
I do
– and understand

Aristotle said, 'For the things we have to learn before we can do them, we learn by doing them.'

To illustrate the practical application of some of the techniques discussed I would like to tell you about Robert.

Robert was a 30-year-old graphic designer who came to see me complaining of panic attacks. They had troubled him for many years and he finally decided to do something about them.

From the first visit it was obvious that he was prepared to put into practice what we had discussed. He approached his treatment like a project he had been set at work. He read the books I suggested, gave time for himself to relax, and took risks in areas that were frightening.

We looked at the various factors relevant to his panics and uncovered a list of negative attitudes.

1. He was a pessimist.
2. He constantly worried in case things went wrong.
3. He worried about other people's problems. (He was a problem thief.)
4. He was anxious about the future (What if . . .?).
5. He lacked confidence and had many doubts about himself.
6. He needed to be liked.
7. He constantly felt guilty.

It seemed likely that the panic attacks were related to these attitudes so we spent a few sessions devising a list of activities to counter these. He agreed to:

1. Spend half an hour sitting quietly by himself in meditation. This meant he was focused internally, allowed thoughts to drift through his mind, allowed his breathing to slow and

become regular, move his attitude from an active 'doing' state to a passive 'being' state.

2. Visualise films in his head showing positive outcomes. This meant using his imagination to see in his mind's eye events that lead to a positive result. He was to look at some event in the future and see it as a film with a happy ending.

3. Continuously repeat a 'mantra' of positive statements about future events.

4. Focus on his own needs and allow others to deal with their difficulties.

Some time later he came to see me with a beaming smile.

'Did you try out some of the things we discussed?' I asked him, knowing that clients often have the best intentions but fail to put them into practice.

'Sure did,' he grinned.

'Tell me about it.'

'I got married last week and it was the best day of my life. For the last month I have been doing the things we discussed. I've taken time every day to relax and visualise a film in my head of the wedding going really well.

I repeated a mantra many times a day telling myself how wonderful the wedding would be. I told myself that the guests' happiness was not my responsibility. We were providing the surroundings for their happiness but it was up to them whether they enjoyed it or not.

I spent time preparing my speech which is unusual for me as I generally leave everything till the last minute. The speech went really well. I felt calm and relaxed when I was giving it, which is amazing for me. Many of my friends said it was the best wedding they had been to. If I had not done the preparation we devised, I'm sure I would have panicked with all that responsibility.'

The look on Robert's face supported every word he said.

Robert illustrates the essential ingredients of this book.

He had long-term problems related to lack of confidence and

negative beliefs. He recognised the problems and decided to do something about them.

He was prepared to listen and take on board what he heard. He put time and effort into converting advice into practical tasks which he carried out daily. He used this learning to ensure he had a happy and successful wedding day.

Robert had many similarities to everyone reading this book. He had most of the underlying difficulties we all have when striving to build our confidence.

You too can make use of the information contained in this book, combine it with your time and effort and achieve a successful outcome for the goals you are seeking.

Some people have forty years of experience to call upon, others have one year of experience repeated forty times.

CONFIDENCE BOOSTERS

- In this chapter Robert epitomised someone who had problems and put in time and effort to resolve them. Many people have the best intentions but are diverted by other needs taking precedence over their aims.

  In order to help improve your confidence, think of *one* aspect of your life that troubles you and concentrate on improving that.

  Formulate your plan by writing down:
  − Your aim
  − How much time you are prepared to put into achieving this aim
  − What time of day would be most suitable
  − A commitment to spending that time on a regular basis
  − What *exactly* you intend to do
  − How you could put this into practical use in everyday life.

For example:
- I want to improve my confidence.
- I need half an hour a day to achieve this.
- It would suit me best when I get home from work and before I have dinner.
- I make that commitment.
- I intend to repeat affirmations, do relaxation on some evenings and read recommended literature on other occasions.
- I will take risks during the day in situations I have previously found frightening or embarrassing.

32

Conclusion

Looking through the chapters of this book, as if fitting pieces in a jigsaw, we can see how the picture of confidence is formed.

Each individual piece contributes to the picture and may represent a smaller or larger portion of the whole. What we end up with is an *attitude* – either 'out there' towards the world or inwardly towards ourselves.

Confidence is represented by this specific attitude depicted by the jigsaw picture. It is not an entity, a thing we can hold up and show people, it is an attitude, a perspective, a way we view the world or ourselves.

This perspective will change when we alter any of its component parts, just as a picture in the jigsaw will change if we alter the position of the pieces.

A major step towards improvement is recognising that the jigsaw (your attitude) is *not reality*, it is just your view of reality, and so can be changed. If your view causes low self-esteem then altering some of the components will improve this and form a more appropriate view of reality.

Each chapter represents a piece of your own specific jigsaw, your own perspective on reality. By choosing those pieces that need adjusting you can focus on specific areas that will improve your confidence.

The case histories show you are not on your own. We all have jigsaws that need improvement. We all have perspectives that distort reality. Your specific difficulties are shared by thousands trying to find solutions. Gain strength from the knowledge you are not on your own; many have trodden your path, carried your fears and made your mistakes.

Allow yourself the good feeling that you are doing something about it, you are taking steps on the journey of control. Putting new ideas into practice is worthy of praise in itself. The more time and energy you put into this project the better the results will be. Gaining support, guidance along the way is also important.

Although, as I've said, your attitude (the jigsaw) is not reality, by improving your attitude you will in fact improve reality. You will notice things you haven't noticed before; you will receive positive responses where previously there were none; you will succeed where previously you failed.

I can assure you the effort is worth it. But that is not enough; you need to find that for yourself. You need to do something differently, receive a positive response and say to yourself, 'He was right', then you know you've taken a major step in the right direction.

It is the 'Aha response', a light turning on inside, a penny dropping, a real realisation that signifies you are on the right track.

In chaos theory it is said that a butterfly landing on a leaf in South America has reverberations all around the world. May I wish for you many butterflies landing all over the world so that the reverberations reflect in your life as a building of confidence and self-esteem.

Further Reading

Virginia Axline, *Dibs In Search Of Self*, Penguin Books

Jean Dominique Bauby, *The Diving Bell and the Butterfly*, Fourth Estate

Deepak Chopra, *The Seven Spiritual Laws Of Success*, Bantam Press

Paulo Coelho, *The Alchemist*, Thorsons

Robert Fulgum, *It Was On Fire When I Lay Down On It*, Grafton Books

Louise Hay, *You Can Heal Your Life* (Affirmations), Eden Grove Editions

Susan Jeffers, *Feel The Fear and Do It Anyway*, Arrow

Gael Lindenfield, *Confident Children*, Thorsons

Anthony de Mello, *Awareness*, Fount Publisher

Monty Roberts, *The Man Who Listens To Horses*, Hutchinson Press